THE
NEW
CIVIL WAR

ACKNOWLEDGMENTS

Many people have provided the support, information, and patience necessary to make this book a reality. At the top of the list is E. Russell Primm. Without his commitment, his belief, and his support, this book would never have been printed. Michael Bradley provided essential and absolutely astonishing help when he simply handed over his lengthy research on lesbian and gay youth. Ben Zimmerman and all the other people of the Freedom Coalition, Simply Equal, and Parents, Families and Friends of Lesbians and Gays (P-FLAG) in Lawrence, Kansas, have done more than they can ever know to make this book possible. The women of my writers' group helped remind me of the importance of my work. Finally, the most important thank-you has to go to my son, Tony, who at nine years old had to suffer through a mom who was working on a manuscript instead of a Halloween costume.

For my son, Tony, and all his friends.
May they learn to think for themselves.

CONTENTS

INTRODUCTION
THE NEW CIVIL WAR   13

CHAPTER 1
**THE STRUGGLE OVER CIVIL RIGHTS
IN THE UNITED STATES   20**
Prejudice, Stereotypes, and Discrimination   33
Comparing Rights   35

CHAPTER 2
INSIDE LESBIAN AND GAY AMERICA   37
A Day in the Life of Lesbian and Gay Kansas   47
A World Without Homosexuality   51
Questions and Answers About Sexual Orientation   52

CHAPTER 3
**BATTLEGROUND:
RELIGION   54**
The Religious Life of Lesbians and Gays   66

CHAPTER 4
**BATTLEGROUND:
DECRIMINALIZING HOMOSEXUALITY   68**
Where Lesbians and Gays Are Criminals   77
Portrait of a Child Molester   78

CHAPTER 5
**BATTLEGROUND:
PROTECTION FROM DISCRIMINATION   80**

CHAPTER 6
BATTLEGROUND:
THE MILITARY   97
The Army's First Official Gay Soldier   109

CHAPTER 7
BATTLEGROUND:
AIDS AND GAY RIGHTS   111
The Face of AIDS   122

CHAPTER 8
BATTLEGROUND:
LESBIAN AND GAY FAMILIES   124
Domestic Partnerships   134

CHAPTER 9
BATTLEGROUND:
LESBIAN AND GAY TEENS   136

CHAPTER 10
THE FUTURE   147

▼ ▼ ▼

GROUPS SUPPORTING
CIVIL RIGHTS   159

GROUPS OPPOSING
CIVIL RIGHTS   161

SOURCE
NOTES   163

FOR MORE
INFORMATION   182

INDEX   187

THE
NEW
CIVIL WAR

THE NEW CIVIL WAR

Not every war is a shooting war. Sometimes wars are fought in legislatures as different sides struggle to pass their versions of a law. Sometimes wars are fought in a courtroom where the result of a lawsuit will lead to great change in society. Sometimes the battles are marches and other public protests as different sides attempt to force their opponents to do what they want. And sometimes the marches, courtroom battles, and legislative debates are only the beginning. At times these nonviolent activities change into violence and a shooting war breaks out.

Today many Americans believe they are in the middle of a war—a new civil war. At the center of the conflict are lesbian and gay Americans and two key questions:

1. Should lesbian and gay citizens have a place in American society?
2. Should lesbian and gay citizens have the same civil rights as heterosexuals?

Although the struggle over civil rights for lesbians and gays used to be confined to a few large cities, today the debate is occurring almost everywhere in the country. In rural Mississippi, for example, heterosexuals are challenging the right of a lesbian couple to live openly and create a retreat for other lesbians. In Oregon, Missouri, Maine, Idaho, Ohio, and many other states, antigay groups have campaigned for proposals that would forever keep lesbians and gays from gaining equal rights with heterosexuals. When the U.S. Supreme Court declared the Colorado proposal unconstitutional, antigay groups vowed to continue the fight. At the same time, Hawaii appears ready to legalize same-sex marriage. In Utah, lesbian, gay, and bisexual teenagers struggle for the right to have a school club. Meanwhile writers sell books about a new "culture war" and some politicians have declared that the nation must fight a "holy war" against homosexuals.[1]

The purpose of this book is to give you the information you need to understand the fight and to make up your own mind about the issues. To do that, the book includes two chapters that provide overviews of the subject of civil rights and lesbians and gays. Seven other chapters detail the issues that are the battlegrounds in this new civil war. Each of the battleground chapters has four sections. The first section lists the major questions that are being debated. The second lists the arguments of both sides in the debate. The third reports the current situation. The fourth provides evidence to help you decide where you stand on the issue. At the end of the book, you will find a list of organizations on both sides of the debate. Addresses and phone numbers are provided so that you can research the issues on your own.

A WORD ABOUT LANGUAGE

Most often this book will refer to homosexuals as lesbian and gay. A lesbian is a female homosexual, and a gay is a male homosexual although sometimes people use the word to mean all homosexuals, including women. This is the current termi-

14

nology used by the major news media and preferred by most American lesbians and gays. (By the way, the term *lesbian* is derived from the Greek island of Lesbos, where a famous female poet, Sappho, wrote love poems to women.) You also must understand several other terms.

Sexual Orientation refers to a person's self-identification as either homosexual, heterosexual, or bisexual.

Homosexual refers to a male or female who finds emotional and sexual fulfillment with members of the same sex.

Heterosexual refers to a male or female who finds emotional and sexual fulfillment with members of the opposite sex.

Bisexual refers to a male or female who finds emotional and sexual fulfillment with members of either sex.

Fag (or Faggot) is a derogatory term for a gay man.

Dyke is a derogatory term for a lesbian.

Queer is a derogatory term for a lesbian or gay man. Recently this word has been reclaimed as a positive term by some lesbians and gay men.

Come Out is a slang expression for acknowledging one's homosexuality to oneself and to others.[2]

OPPONENTS

The most active opponents of civil rights for lesbians and gays are usually affiliated with the most conservative churches in the United States. They include TV evangelist Pat Robertson, who founded the Christian Coalition; James Dobson of Focus on the Family, Lou Sheldon of the Traditional Values Coalition, Donald Wildmon of the American Family Association, Phyllis Schafley of Eagle Forum, and Beverly LaHaye of Concerned Women for America. Other opponents include media commentator and Republican presidential candidate Pat Buchanan, Senator Jesse Helms (R–North Carolina), and Representative Robert Dornan (R–California). Here is what a few of the opponents say:

Homosexuals are sexually troubled people engaging in dangerous activities. Because we care about them and those tempted to join them, it is important that we neither encourage nor legitimize such a destructive lifestyle.[3]

Paul Cameron
Family Research Institute

Judaism sees the family as the bedrock of sane society, and understands homosexuality to be the family's most lethal enemy.[4]

Rabbi Shlomo Riskin

I'm inclined to the view that fags, deep-dyed fags, can't be saved. God has given them up. . . . They're murderous liars, as the Lord Jesus called them, capable of any violence. Their dominant characteristics are murder and lies.[5]

The Rev. Fred Phelps of the Westboro
Baptist Church of Topeka, Kansas

Gay rights enacted into law becomes tyranny for those who favor traditional sexual morality.

Robert H. Knight, director of cultural studies
Family Research Council

What the gays are asking here is a government seal of approval on this life style. . . . You can't equate race and sex-

ual orientation because that identifies someone who takes account of sexual orientation with racial bigotry.[6]

Michael Carvin, a Washington, D.C.,
attorney engaged in an antigay lawsuit

Most of society is willing to tolerate a subculture built around a homosexual life style. What we want to do is establish a barrier. The state must ultimately say that homosexuality is wrong.[7]

Lon Mabin,
founder of Oregon Citizens Alliance

Please remember, homosexuals do not reproduce! They recruit! And many of them are out after my children and your children. . . . Let me repeat, a massive homosexual revolution can bring the judgement of God upon this nation.[8]

Jerry Falwell, evangelist

SUPPORTERS

Supporters of civil rights for lesbians and gay men include both heterosexuals and homosexuals, individuals and organizations. Among the most well-known supporters are Barry Goldwater, a conservative former U.S. senator and a onetime presidential candidate. Other supporters include the Reverend Jesse Jackson, a civil rights activist, and entertainers Tom Hanks, Whoopi Goldberg, and Barbra Streisand. Among the supportive organizations are *The New York Times, USA Today*, and the NAACP, which was one of the leading groups that helped win civil rights for African-Americans. Other supporters include many church organizations, such as Unitarian Universalists, United Church of Christ, United Methodist Church, and the Episcopal Diocese of Washington, D.C. Here is what just a few of the supporters say:

Discrimination against people because of their sexual orientation is wrong and unacceptable. My husband, Martin Luther King Jr. said, "I have worked too long and hard against segregated public accommodations to end up segregating my moral concerns. Justice is indivisible."

Coretta Scott King, civil rights leader and widow of
slain civil rights leader, Dr. Martin Luther King Jr.

This is my message to political leaders in every jurisdiction in this country: We cannot be silent in the face of hatred, we cannot be accepting in the face of bigotry, we cannot be apathetic in the wake of violence. We must speak up, we must stand up, and our numbers will multiply.[9]

Former Oregon governor Barbara Roberts

What do you mean by "natural"? If you say "natural" in terms of how people love each other, then who cares if the relationship is gay or straight as long as the love can be expressed and received? That is what's natural—not to be able to love is what's unnatural.[10]

Reverend William Sloan Coffin Jr.

I am both gay and conservative and don't find a contradiction. There shouldn't be any "shame" in being gay. Moreover, the conservative view, based as it is on the inherent rights of the individual over the state, is the logical political home of gay men and women.[11]

Marvin Liebman, one of the founders of
the modern conservative movement

Freezing gays out of equal opportunities offends the nation's most basic principles.[12]

USA Today

The antigay movement in Kansas City isn't new, but it's growing. . . . Their excuses for intolerance are remindful of so-called God-fearing whites who objected to civil rights laws in the 1960s. People said then that steps must be taken to ensure racial purity, protect their children, heritage and family values from uncivilized people of savage races. Homosexuals are seen as a similar threat, even as a public health menace. . . . In Oregon, Colorado and elsewhere, sweeping antigay initiatives are on state ballots. If concerned citizens aren't careful, it could happen here. Homosexuality isn't contagious. Hatred is.[13]

Kansas City Star

CHAPTER 1

THE STRUGGLE OVER CIVIL RIGHTS IN THE UNITED STATES

A REVOLUTIONARY CONCEPT

The concept of civil rights is relatively new in human history. It means that all people in a society have equal legal rights. No one person or group of people or even the government is supposed to control people's lives. Until the last half the 20th century, equality under the law was not the law in most of the world.[1] Even the birthplace of democracy, ancient Athens, did not have a true democracy that included equal civil rights for all. Only men who were citizens of Athens enjoyed full civil rights. Women and slaves had no voice and no vote in the running of the city.

When Europeans came to North America, people were beginning to believe that the power of government should be limited. By the time the thirteen colonies were under the control of the English king, people in England were beginning to enjoy some rights. For example, the British version of Congress, the Parliament, gave English citizens a voice in government.

Despite the progress made in English law, the civil rights of the colonists in the New World were severely limited. Parliament passed laws affecting the American colonies, yet not a single colonist had a vote in Parliament. Customs inspectors could enter and search people's homes at any time, even if there was no evidence that a law had been broken. The press was censored by government. Colonists came to believe that no one in England would help them. In 1776, the colonies declared their independence from England and soon found themselves fighting a war.

▼ ▼ ▼

The American victory in the Revolutionary War led to freedom from England, but it also left Americans with a new problem. How should they govern themselves? What rights should people have in the new society? At first, the newly free states believed that the only way to preserve individual freedom was to keep government weak. In 1781, they adopted the Articles of Confederation, which gave little power to the central government. Six years later, however, Americans realized that the Confederation was not working.

In 1787, George Washington, James Madison, Benjamin Franklin, Alexander Hamilton, and 51 other men met in Philadelphia to try again. This time they succeeded in creating the document that would become the foundation of our society. When they wrote the Constitution, however, they left out the Bill of Rights.

The lack of a Bill of Rights almost derailed the campaign to ratify the Constitution. In several states, the Constitution was only approved after people were promised that a Bill of Rights would be added to the Constitution at the first meeting of Congress. In 1789, James Madison kept that promise. Then a member of the newly formed U.S. House of Representatives, Madison introduced the Bill of Rights as amendments to the Constitution. Taken from several state constitutions, the amendments provided many protections, including freedom of religion, speech, press, and assembly. They banned general searches and recognized that even people accused of crimes have rights. By 1791, the Bill of Rights had been ratified by two-thirds of the existing 14 states. They became the first ten amendments to the Constitution.

The ratification of the Bill of Rights completed the first stage in the struggle over civil rights in America.[2] The U.S. Constitution marked a revolution in human history because it did more than just create a new government. It changed the purpose of government. Before it was adopted, the role of government was to enforce the community's ideas on its citizens and to protect them from threats to their safety. Under this role, government's job was to make certain its citizens followed the state-approved religion and the state-approved version of truth. Thomas Jefferson, James Madison, and the other founders of the United States wanted to do something much different. To them, the primary job of government was to protect people's rights. Government was still expected to protect people against threats to their safety, but it was not supposed to tell people how to live. On the contrary, the founders meant to protect citizens by preventing government from interfering with their lives. In a very real sense, the U.S. Constitution was a triumph of freedom.

A FLAWED TRIUMPH

The U.S. Constitution was also a flawed triumph. Created by a society that kept slaves, the Constitution reflected the prejudices of the times. In fact, the Constitution originally left out more people than it included. As originally written, the only people who were truly equal in the Constitution were white men who owned property. They were the only group that could vote and fully participate in government. Poor white men had no vote. Women could not vote; if they were married, women were legally classified as the property of their husbands. Native Americans had an even more difficult time. They were considered an alien people who were not covered by the laws of the United States. With none of the protections of the Bill of Rights, Native Americans were treated like enemies. In 1838, for example, the U.S. Army drove the Cherokee out of their homes in Georgia and Tennessee. In what became known as the Trail of Tears, 15,000 Cherokee were forced to walk to Arkansas and what is now Oklahoma. About 4,000 died of disease and exposure along the way.[3]

Perhaps the greatest failure of the Founding Fathers was their treatment of African-Americans and the institution of slavery. At the same time that the delegates to the Constitutional Convention claimed to be creating a government based on freedom, they ignored pleas to ban slavery. Instead, the Constitutional Convention put endorsements of slavery in three places in the Constitution and counted slaves as less than fully human. The Constitution declared that each slave equaled three-fifths of a person for the purposes of determining taxes and representation in Congress.

When Rhode Island became the last state to ratify the Constitution in 1790, the stage was set for centuries of struggle. The center of that struggle was and is the great contradiction in American society. Despite the fact that our nation was founded on the belief that all people are "created equal," there have always been groups of people who were not equal. At times, these groups have been imprisoned, deprived of jobs, and kept from adequate education and housing. Sometimes people have not even been allowed to get a cup of coffee at a lunch counter or sit in the front of a bus.

THE AFRICAN-AMERICAN STRUGGLE

The modern concept of civil rights was pioneered by African-Americans in their long struggle to become full citizens of the United States.[4] Although the first Africans to come to colonial America were not slaves, the slave trade was thriving in the colonies by 1660. Despite slave rebellions, the Underground Railroad, and the efforts of the antislavery Abolitionist Movement, the institution of slavery persisted until after the Civil War.

The first blow against slavery came from the pen of President Abraham Lincoln when he issued the Emancipation Proclamation in 1862. Although it was an important step toward freedom, the Emancipation Proclamation was only the first step. The Proclamation only freed slaves in Confederate states. This left 80,000 people in slavery in the southern border states that had not left the Union when the rest of the South left to form the Confederacy. Slavery was not finally abolished until the 13th Amendment to the Constitution was ratified on December 18, 1865.

For a brief time after the Civil War, African-Americans had a taste of freedom. They voted and held public office. Two African-Americans were elected to the U.S. Senate and twenty were elected to the U.S. House. But only two years after the end of the Civil War, a new war began in the South that would take away the freedom of African-Americans. This was a guerrilla war of terror and intimidation designed to keep African-Americans from taking their place as equals in American society. Secret groups such as the Ku Klux Klan began what they saw as a "holy crusade." African-Americans were beaten, whipped, or lynched if they tried to exercise their rights. African-American officials were forced to resign their offices. In just the first two years of the twentieth century, more than two hundred African-Americans were lynched.

By 1875, slavery supporters in state legislatures passed laws to limit the freedom of African-Americans. Known as segregation laws, these measures made African-Americans second-class citizens by keeping them separate from whites and denying them the right to vote. Under these laws, African-Americans were forced to live in separate neighborhoods, go to separate schools, and eat in different restaurants if allowed in restaurants at all. They were forced into the lowest-paying jobs. They could not even drink out of the same water fountain as whites.

In 1896, the U.S. Supreme Court upheld the constitutionality of these laws in the case of *Plessy v. Ferguson*. The court declared that the laws were constitutional as long as the separate facilities for African-Americans were equal to those of whites.

Although African-Americans made progress in the next fifty years, segregation was not broken until the Civil Rights Movement of the 1950s and 1960s. In 1954, the U.S. Supreme Court gave African-Americans the legal lever they needed when the high court declared segregation to be unconstitutional in the *Brown v. Board of Education* case. Two years later, the bus boycott in Montgomery, Alabama, forced the city to end segregation on public transportation. Through sit-ins, boycotts, voter-registration drives, marching, and organizing, African-Americans eventually smashed the segregation laws. They also won important changes in the law. Although these new laws did not end prejudice, they did take away the legal support for discrimination. These new laws also established the legal principle that all people should be treated fairly by both the government and private individuals.

The African-American Civil Rights Movement gave birth to many other civil rights movements in the 1960s. African-Americans not only made new law, their success gave new hope. Among the many efforts sparked by the African-American Civil Rights Movement were the efforts to end discrimination against women, Hispanic Americans, Native Americans, Asian-Americans, people with disabilities, and lesbians and gays.

THE STATUS OF LESBIANS AND GAYS THROUGHOUT HISTORY

The legal status of lesbians and gays has varied throughout history. At times homosexuals enjoyed the support of their society. In ancient Greece, for example, love between males was common and honored. Some historians also believe the early Christian church tolerated homosexuality and performed same-sex marriages.[5]

That attitude began to change, however, around the fourth century about the time Christianity became the official state religion of the Roman Empire. As Rome took more control over people's personal lives, the death penalty was imposed on homosexuals.

After the fall of the Roman Empire many minorities, including lesbians and gays, found acceptance in parts of Europe. From the seventh century to the middle of the twelfth century, homosexuals, Jews, and other minorities lived freely in many countries. Some even attained high social positions. By the last half of the twelfth century, however, intolerance had returned to Europe. For many centuries to follow, lesbians and gays were punished. They were maimed and executed, often killed by being burned alive. When Europeans settled the Americas, the death penalty for homosexuality came with them.

While some people have sought to punish homosexuals, others have tried to cure them. The "treatments" have often been brutal. At times, these treatments looked no different from punishments. Treatments included castration, hysterectomy, and surgical removal of a woman's ovaries and clitoris. Also used were shock therapy, which involves shocking the patient with electricity and can cause permanent physical and mental damage. Lobotomies to cure homosexuality were performed as late as 1951. (A lobotomy is a form of brain surgery that can rob an individual of the ability to act, feel, and even think clearly.) Even in modern times the "cure" could be deadly. British physicians reported in 1964 that one of their patients suffered a heart attack and died from their therapy. Their cure consisted of giving him drugs to make him nauseous while he talked about homosexuality. Reports of the use of electric shock and the use of nausea-inducing drugs continued to surface in the 1990s.[6]

One of the most desperate times for homosexuals came during Nazi influence in Germany.[7] Even before they controlled the German government, Nazis attacked people organizing for lesbian and gay rights. In 1920, Nazis interrupted and beat participants at a meeting on the issue. In 1921, Nazi youths carrying guns opened fire on people attending a committee lecture in Vienna, wounding many people in the audience. One of the first book burnings by the Nazis destroyed more than 10,000 books about homosexuality at the Institute for Sex Research.

One of the reasons the Nazi party finally won a majority of the seats in the German parliament in 1933 was that they called for "moral purity." The Nazi campaign platform emphasized racial and sexual "purity," rigid sex roles where men had one set of duties and women another, and an idealized view of the heterosexual family. Immediately after the 1933 election, Nazis intensified their campaign against homosexuals. In 1935, the Nazis expanded the scope of Germany's existing antigay laws to imprison people for hugging, kissing, or even having homosexual fantasies. A year later, Heinrich Himmler, chief of the Gestapo (the German secret police), called for homosexuals to be put to death. He said:

> As National Socialists [Nazis] we are not afraid to fight against this plague within our own ranks. Just as we have readopted the ancient Germanic approach to the question of marriage between alien races, so too, in our judgment of homosexuality—a symptom of racial degeneracy destructive to our race—we have returned to the guiding Nordic principle that degenerates should be exterminated. Germany stands or falls with the purity of its race.[8]

Like Jews,[9] gypsies, political opponents, and other groups, lesbians and gays were rounded up by the Nazis and imprisoned in concentration camps. In the camps, the inmates, including homosexuals, were tortured, starved, worked to death, beaten to death, hanged, and shot. The concentration-camp prisoners were classified by the different patches they wore. Jews wore a yellow star. Gays wore pink triangles placed point down. Today, many lesbians and gays have adopted the pink triangle as a symbol of the fight for civil rights.

No one knows how many homosexuals were murdered by the Nazis. One estimate gives a figure of 200,000 while another estimate says the number was 10,000. Other historians have argued that the number of dead, while important, is not as important as the horror they suffered. When the concentration camps were liberated, the United States and their Allies freed the surviving Jews, political prisoners, and other heterosexuals who had been kept captive. Feeling that imprisonment of homosexuals was justifiable, the Allies returned gays to prison to "serve out the remainder of their sentences."[10] Soon after the war ended, Germany paid money to heterosexual concentration-camp survivors to help repair their suffering. Germany did not pay reparations to surviving gay victims of the concentration camps until 1982.

THE LESBIAN AND GAY CIVIL RIGHTS MOVEMENT

The movement for civil rights for lesbians and gays began more than a century ago in Germany. The first known protests against repressive German laws occurred as early as 1869. Nearly thirty years later, the Scientific Humanitarian Committee was organized to fight the antigay laws in Germany. The earliest documented gay rights group in the United States was the Society for Human Rights, which was organized in Chicago in 1924.

Lesbian and gay organizations did not become active in the United States, however, until after World War II. Henry Hay founded the Mattachine Society in Los Angeles in 1948. One Inc. formed in Los Angeles in 1953. Both organizations were primarily for gay men. Del Martin and Phyllis Lyon founded a group for lesbians called Daughters of Bilitis in 1955 in San Francisco. Before long, chapters had been organized in New York, Los Angeles, and twelve other cities. Because of the repression of the time, all of these groups used names that gave no hint that they were organizations of lesbians and gays.

The postwar era was difficult for homosexuals. Labeled as "perverts" by Senator Joseph McCarthy and his Communist-hunting colleagues, gays and lesbians were officially classified as a threat to national security. Homosexuals were actively hunted and fired from any government job. Between 2,000 and 3,000 lesbians and gays were fired every year from federal jobs. During this period, homosexuals had little or no support from anyone but themselves. Even organizations such as the American Civil Liberties Union, which championed rights for other minorities, refused to help. Meanwhile, the press was filled with stories about gay conspiracies and called homosexuality the "New Moral Menace to Our Youth."[11]

With no support and no laws banning discrimination, few lesbians and gays fought back. A sense of outrage, however, was beginning to build. By 1965, the first civil rights demonstrations had been held. Groups of twenty to thirty lesbians and gays picketed the United Nations, the White House, Independence Hall in Philadelphia, and the headquarters of federal agencies. With men dressed in suits and ties and women in dresses and blouses and skirts, the picketers looked no different than anyone else on the street. But the real explosion would not come for another four years.

The spark that ignited that explosion was a routine police raid on a gay bar in New York called the Stonewall Inn. For decades gay bars had been the only places where lesbians and gays could meet and socialize. For decades police had been harassing the bars. As early as 1923, a New York City ordinance allowed police to arrest and fine anyone who participated in "degenerate disorderly conduct," which included same-sex dancing or even a touch between people of the same sex. Sometimes police would simply come into a bar and question patrons. Other times police would drive a paddy wagon up to the door, burst in, and arrest everyone inside. Bar patrons would run, but they would not resist.

On June 27, 1969, everything changed. When police arrived at the Stonewall Inn, gays and lesbians fought back. They drove off the police that night and held them off for a second night. Although the events at Stonewall did not change any laws, they did change the way lesbians and gays thought of themselves. Stonewall helped many realize that they could fight back, and sometimes they could even win.

Within a month of what came to be known as the Stonewall Rebellion, activist organizations began meeting. On the one-year anniversary of the Stonewall Rebellion, the first gay pride march was held in New York City. Thousands marched, carrying signs reading, among other things: "Lesbians Unite," "Homosexual Is Not a Four-Letter Word," "Gay Power," and "I Am a Lesbian and I Am Beautiful."[12]

The first legal successes of the lesbian and gay movement came in the 1970s, 1980s, and 1990s. One of the earliest successes occurred on December 15, 1973, when the American Psychiatric Association Board of Trustees voted 13–0 to remove homosexuality from its official list of mental illnesses. Four months later, 4,854 of the association's members—58 percent of those voting—ratified the board's decision in a secret ballot. The same year, the American Bar Association adopted a resolution urging states to repeal all antigay sex laws.

Activists also won passage of the first laws protecting lesbian and gay citizens from discrimination. Most antidiscrimination laws were passed in cities and counties, including Wichita, Kansas; St. Paul, Minnesota; Boulder, Colorado; Cincinnati, Ohio; and Dade County, Florida. In 1982, Wisconsin became the first state in the nation to pass an antidiscrimination law.

As lesbian and gay citizens won victories, opposition grew. Passage of the civil rights law in Dade County prompted former beauty queen Anita Bryant to launch an anti-gay-rights campaign she called "Save Our Children." Bryant's campaign succeeded in overturning civil rights laws in Miami, Wichita, St. Paul, and in many other cities in the late 1970s.

The most damaging blow to lesbian and gay civil rights came in 1986 when the U.S. Supreme Court voted 5–4 in the *Bowers v. Hardwick* case to uphold the constitutionality of sodomy laws. These are the laws that make it a crime for adult lesbians and gays to have sex in their own homes. The ruling and its impact are discussed in detail in Chapter 5.

THE SITUATION TODAY

As the twenty-first century dawns, the battle over civil rights for lesbians and gays continues. Lesbian and gay Americans have won many victories. The U.S. Supreme Court has declared antigay measures that prohibit lesbians and gays from trying to win passage of civil rights laws to be unconstitutional. More than one hundred cities, towns, and counties have passed civil rights protection for lesbians and gays. Nine states protect against discrimination against lesbians and gays.

Meanwhile, opponents have also won successes. A federal ban on same-sex marriages has become law. Similar bans on same-sex marriages have also been passed in several states. Opponents succeeded in blocking an effort to end the ban on gays in the military. Despite the fact that they were later overturned by the Supreme Court, antigay groups also won symbolic victories when they convinced voters in Colorado, Cincinnati, and several other places to approve measures banning civil rights protection for homosexuals.

Little is certain about the future of the debate. As lesbians, gays, and their heterosexual supporters continue to march and organize, opponents continue to do the same. Every civil rights victory leads to opposition. Every opposition victory leads to renewed efforts by civil rights supporters. At this point, no one can predict which side will win. All that appears certain is that the struggle over civil rights for lesbians and gays will not end soon.

PREJUDICE, STEREOTYPES, AND DISCRIMINATION

One factor has remained the same in the long struggle over civil rights in the United States. The discrimination faced by each minority group has been an outgrowth of prejudice.[13] Today lesbian and gay Americans say that they, too, are the victims of prejudice. Meanwhile, their opponents claim that prejudice is not the issue. Instead, opponents say that homosexuals are different from heterosexuals and, therefore, should not be given the same civil rights that heterosexuals enjoy. How can you decide which side is telling the truth? The first step is to understand the key concepts of prejudice, stereotypes, and discrimination.

The Latin root of the word *prejudice* means "prejudgment." To feel prejudice toward a person or a group is to have a negative opinion of them without reason or before getting sufficient information to make an informed opinion. People can be prejudiced against a group without ever having met a member of the group.

Stereotypes are both the content of prejudiced thinking and the fuel that keeps prejudice going. A *stereotype* is a myth that says all people in a certain group behave exactly the same way and have the same traits. Sometimes a stereotype may contain a small element of truth, but that tiny truth is exaggerated and distorted. Most often, stereotypes have no foundation in fact. When people are prejudiced, they think in terms of stereotypes, they teach their children stereotypes, and they use stereotypes to justify their actions against minority groups.

In the United States, stereotypes have been used against many minority groups. For example, African-

33

Americans have been stereotyped as mentally inferior, violent, unstable, and carriers of disease. Stereotypes of Jews portray them as being sly, dishonest, money-hungry people who carry sexual diseases. Asians have been stereotyped as being sly and tricky. Meanwhile, lesbians and gays are seen as being of low moral character, being promiscuous, carrying disease, acting as sexual predators, and being violent and mentally ill.

One key component of most stereotypes involves sexuality. This occurs despite the fact that the identifying factors of most minority groups are nonsexual, such as skin color and religion. Most often, the minority group is portrayed as promiscuous, diseased, and child molesters. For example, Nazi leader Adolf Hitler accused Jews of being a public health threat because he claimed they were sexual predators who carried sexually transmitted diseases.

Stereotypes are difficult to change. People tend to cling to them even when they are given proof the stereotypes are wrong. People do this by remembering the information that confirms their prejudices and ignoring information that contradicts them. To hold on to a prejudice, people will even admit that some individuals may not fit the stereotypes for the group and then declare that exceptions mean nothing.

The end result of prejudice and stereotypes is discrimination, which occurs when people are treated differently because they are members of a minority group. Discrimination can be written into the laws of the land. Examples of this form of discrimination include the segregation laws that once kept African-Americans from eating in the same restaurants and living in the same neighborhoods as white Americans. Even if laws are changed, however, people's attitudes can still lead to discrimination. For example, African-Americans may be turned down for a job at a predominantly white company because they don't "look right" to the company executives.

COMPARING RIGHTS

	Heterosexual	Homosexual
Freedom of speech	yes	no
Right to marry, including right to: • visit spouse in hospital • inherit property from spouse • participate in family medical insurance	yes	no
Equal pay for equal work	yes	no
Custody of own children	yes	no
Adopt and/or foster children	yes	no
Sexual relations with adult partner in the privacy of home	yes	no
Serve in the military	yes	no
Protection from discrimination based on sexual orientation in: • employment • housing • public accommodation like restaurants and stores	no	no

COMPARING RIGHTS

Under the current laws of the United States, heterosexual and homosexual Americans do not have the same rights. There is no city, county, or state in the nation where lesbian and gay citizens have equal rights with heterosexual citizens.

For example, the First Amendment right to freedom of speech does not apply to lesbians and gays when they serve in the military. If a gay man does nothing more than tell a friend that he had a same-sex date, he can be thrown out of the U. S. Army, Navy, Marine Corps, Air Force, or Coast Guard. In all but a handful of cities and states, lesbians and gay men can be fired for mentioning their partners at work.

No state legalizes same-sex marriages. Among other things, this means family benefits, such as medical insurance are denied to lesbian or gay partners. Without the financial advantages of these family benefits, lesbian and gay employees earn less than heterosexuals doing the same job. This applies everywhere except in the companies that offer equal benefits to what they call "domestic partners." Although lesbian mothers and gay fathers have been allowed to keep custody of their children in many places, it isn't universal; there are places in the United States where they have lost custody because of their sexual orientation. The best interests of the child and the parenting abilities of the lesbian mother or gay father have often been ignored by the courts.

One area of the law, however, does treat heterosexuals and homosexuals the same. Protection against discrimination based on sexual orientation is denied to both groups except for the few places that have passed antidiscrimination laws. In the nine states and approximately one hundred cities that have passed antidiscrimination laws, the laws cover both homosexuals and heterosexuals.

CHAPTER 2
INSIDE LESBIAN AND GAY AMERICA

Perhaps the most surprising thing about lesbian and gay America is how ordinary it is. On any given day, lesbian and gay Americans do what other Americans do. They get up, make breakfast, and go to work. They do their laundry. They help their children with their homework. They watch TV, go to the movies, and play softball.

In northeast Kansas, for example, a group of lesbian and gay parents meet once a month to talk over coffee about the difficulties of raising children in the TV age. In Missouri, gay men and lesbians who own small businesses meet to discuss the problems of marketing a pet shop or running a real-estate agency. Lesbian and gay ministers prepare Sunday services for the 1,400-member congregation of the Cathedral of Hope in Dallas. The church is Christian, somewhat conservative in its approach to the Bible, and a member of a primarily lesbian and gay denomination called the Universal Fellowship of Metropolitan Community Churches.

Although San Francisco and New York City are famous for having large lesbian and gay communities, homosexual America does not stop at the boundaries of big cities. Homosexuals live in every state of the union. They live in rural Mississippi and small-town Indiana. They live on ranches in Texas and in the hills of Missouri. Lincoln, Nebraska, has a thriving lesbian community. Oklahoma City, Fort Worth, Texas, and Phoenix, Arizona, host rodeos for lesbian and gay participants. Indianapolis has a lesbian and gay community center called The Diversity Center.

Lesbians and gays come from every ethnic group, every economic class, and every political party. They work every kind of job. Lesbians and gays in Topeka, Kansas, celebrated National Coming Out Day in October one year by publishing their names and occupations in an advertisement in the local newspaper. The "It's OK to Be Gay" ad listed the names of teachers, attorneys, veterinarians, law students, psychotherapists, ministers, librarians, store managers, nurses, and a policy analyst for the Kansas State Legislature.[1]

Journalist Randy Shilts reported that at least one gay man has been in the astronaut program. Among the gays in the military are one U.S. Army four-star general who led one of the most crucial military missions of the 1980s. The Marine Corps has included at least one gay person at four-star rank since 1981, and at least one gay man served on the Joint Chiefs of Staff during the same period. A gay man has navigated the president's airplane, *Air Force One*. Gay sailors have dived with the Navy SEALS. A gay admiral commanded a fleet in recent times, while gay soldiers have worn the green beret of the Special Forces.[2]

An increasing number of lesbians and gays are serving in public office. Some members of Congress, both Republicans and Democrats, are openly homosexual, including representative Barney Frank (D–Massachusetts) and former Representative Steve Gunderson (R–Wisconsin). Among the other acknowledged lesbians and gays serving in public office are city council members in Seattle and legislators in Minnesota, Texas, Missouri, and Oregon. Perhaps the most famous openly lesbian lawmaker is Harvard Law School graduate Sheila James Kuehl, who starred as Zelda Gilroy in the TV comedy "The

Many Loves of Dobie Gillis" from 1959 to 1963. When she won election in 1994, she became the first openly lesbian or gay candidate to win a seat in the California state legislature.

Lesbian and gay families are as diverse as heterosexual families. Some lesbians and gays consider themselves to be married and live happily together for decades. Many times they are parted only by death. Other lesbian and gay couples attempt those kinds of relationships, but they fail, just like the approximately 50 percent of heterosexual couples whose marriages end in divorce. Some lesbians and gays are promiscuous, just like some heterosexuals are promiscuous. Some lesbians and gays have children and some don't.

Although it is impossible to know the exact figure, two different estimates put the number of lesbian and gay parents in the United States at four to five million. An estimated eight to fourteen million children are currently being raised in lesbian or gay households. Lesbians and gays become parents in exactly the same way as heterosexuals. Many conceive children in heterosexual relationships they had before they realized they were homosexual. Other lesbians and gays participate in raising the children of their partners in the same way that heterosexual stepparents do. Some adopt children. Like heterosexual women, lesbians sometimes use alternative insemination to conceive a child.[3]

The children of lesbian and gay families play baseball, build models, play video games, and get good grades or bad grades, just like the children of heterosexual families. Studies show that children raised in lesbian and gay households are no more likely to have problems—and no less likely to have problems—than children raised in heterosexual families.

While civil rights opponents claim that there is one gay lifestyle and that it is evil and destructive, researchers report that the claim is simply not true. There is no one gay lifestyle, just like there is no one heterosexual way of living. Author Eric Marcus discusses the issue in his book *Is It a Choice?*:

> *Not long ago, just after I became single for the first time in nearly a decade, a woman friend of mine told me that she was worried I'd go out and lead a wild "gay lifestyle, Marcus wrote." I knew what my friend was talking about. What she feared was that I would go out dancing all night at gay clubs, drink too much, take drugs, probably take my shirt off when things got too hot, and maybe even have unsafe sex in the balcony overlooking the dance floor. After watching the countless news reports and occasional documentaries over the years about gay people—gay men mostly—the popular image of gay life that has been seared into the minds of most Americans is the urban, single night life led by some gay men—and plenty of straight people as well—during the 1970s. I explained to my concerned friend that my idea of a fun Saturday night now, just as it was a decade ago, is getting the early edition of The New York Times and curling up with the Real Estate section. "Why," I asked her, "would I do in my mid-thirties what I had no desire to do in my mid-twenties?"*[4]

THE SIZE OF LESBIAN AND GAY AMERICA

One of the most controversial topics surrounding lesbian and gay America is its size. Studies have set the number of lesbians and gays in the United States between about 1 percent and 10 percent of the total population. The most famous studies were done by Alfred Kinsey and his associates in the late 1940s and early 1950s. Kinsey estimated the number of lesbians and gays to be as high as 10 percent of the population. Researchers in the 1990s, however, said their studies showed that the number of gays and lesbians was much smaller, perhaps even as low as 1.4 percent of women and 2.8 percent of men. What happened? Was Kinsey wrong, are the new studies wrong, or did millions of gay and lesbian Americans vanish sometime between the 1950s Kinsey project and the 1990s?

The answers to those questions are not simple, but many researchers agree on three points. First, they say that Kinsey's findings were misinterpreted. Kinsey actually found that many Americans had homosexual experiences, but that few, actually only about 4 percent, were "exclusively homosexual." This percentage is roughly comparable to the percentage of Jews in the United States.

Second, the numbers change as the definition of homosexuality changes with each study. For example, if homosexuality is defined as either feeling attraction to the same gender or as having sex with someone of the same gender, then more than 18 percent of men and more than 17 percent of women surveyed in a Harvard study qualify as being gay and lesbian.[5] If, however, homosexuality is defined as being willing to tell a researcher that you are lesbian, gay, or bisexual, then only 1.4 percent of women and 2.8 percent of men are homosexual according to a University of Chicago study.[6]

Finally, all the studies could be underestimating the numbers of lesbians and gays because many—perhaps even most—lesbians and gays hide their sexual orientation from their employers, families, and sometimes even friends. Today many researchers say there is no way to answer the question: How many gays are there? But perhaps the more important question is: Why should the size of the population matter? If civil rights are important for all people, then the size of the group should not enter the debate.

THE CAUSE OF HOMOSEXUALITY

Another central issue in the debate over civil rights for lesbians and gays is the question of how an individual's sexual orientation is determined. Civil rights opponents often argue that homosexuality is a choice, a preference. Because it is a choice, opponents say, lesbians and gays should not be given the same civil rights protection as racial minorities who have no choice about their skin color.

Although the scientific debate about the exact origin of sexual orientation has not been resolved, researchers agree that human beings do not make a conscious decision to become either heterosexual or homosexual. Several recent studies have provided evidence that homosexuality is biologically determined. Scientists at many well-respected institutions such as the National Cancer Institute, the Salk Institute for Biological Studies in San Diego, and McMaster University in Canada have found evidence of this.

Since 1985 at least six scientific studies have found evidence of a "gay gene." These studies looked at twins and discovered that lesbians and gays were more likely than heterosexuals to have lesbian and gay siblings. The highest numbers of lesbian and gay siblings were in identical twins.[7] Other researchers have found differences in the brains of homosexual and heterosexual men. One study found that a key passageway between two parts of the brain may be larger in gays than in heterosexual men.[8]

WHAT MAKES LESBIAN AND GAY AMERICA DIFFERENT

Although the lives of lesbian and gay Americans are not much different from the lives of heterosexual Americans, they do differ in three important areas. First, lesbians and gays go through a process known as "coming out" when they become aware that their sexual orientation is different from the orientation of the majority. Second, lesbians and gays face discrimination. Third, they face violence because of their orientation.

Although sexual orientation may be set as early as the age of three, most lesbians and gays do not become aware that they are homosexual until they are teenagers or adults. Some men and women have not acknowledged their homosexual orientation until they have been in heterosexual marriages for decades and raised children. Some lesbians and gays have not come out until they were in their sixties or seventies.

Because heterosexuality is the norm in the United States, young lesbians and gays may sense that they are somehow different, but not understand how. Even if they do realize that they are homosexual, they face a hostile world. Parents assume their children are heterosexual and may even be hostile to lesbians and gays. TV and movies most often portray lesbians and gays as sick and criminal or simply as miserable and dying. Friends may make antigay jokes or harass anyone who is known to be homosexual. Faced with this hostility, every lesbian and gay American is faced with a choice that never confronts heterosexuals. Lesbians and gays must choose one of three paths:

1. They can deny their sexual orientation to themselves and to others. Psychologists report that this kind of self-denial can cause psychological problems.
2. They can lead double lives. Because most gay people can easily pass in heterosexual society, they can decide to pretend to be heterosexual in public and lead lesbian and gay lives in private. In slang terms,

43

this is known as "being closeted" (as if you were hiding in a closet).

3. They can "come out of the closet" and be honest with themselves and others about their sexual orientation.

Although the process of coming out varies from person to person, researchers have identified common similarities in people's experiences. Several models of coming out have been discussed by researchers. One model identifies six stages in the process:[9]

1. Identity Confusion. The individual feels different, but is uncertain about his or her identity.

2. Identity Comparison. The individual may rationalize his or her difference and believe that it is "only a stage."

3. Identity Tolerance. The individual believes that he or she is "probably gay" and contacts other homosexuals to counteract feelings of isolation and alienation. The person tolerates but does not fully accept identity as a homosexual. At the same time, the individual feels different and separate from heterosexuals.

4. Identity Acceptance. Contact with homosexuals increases. Friendships start to form. The individual sees other lesbians and gays more positively and accepts rather than tolerates a homosexual self-image.

5. Identity Pride. This stage is characterized by the feeling that "these are my people." The individual becomes aware of society's rejection of homosexuals and feels anger at heterosexuals. The individual may also devalue heterosexual institutions like marriage.

6. Identity Synthesis. Anger against heterosexuals lessens as the individual realizes that some heterosexuals are supportive and can be trusted. Although the individual retains a deep sense of pride in being homosexual, he or she sees less of a difference between the homosexual and heterosexual worlds.

The second major difference between homosexual and heterosexual Americans involves discrimination. Civil rights opponents argue that this is a good thing. Opponents say lesbians and gays should be treated differently than heterosexuals. In most cities and states and in many areas of federal law, opponents have gotten their way. As discussed in detail in Chapters 3 through 9, lesbian and gay citizens are legally discriminated against in practically every aspect of life. Something as simple as talking to a coworker can lead to discrimination. Even if people try to challenge that discrimination in court, they can lose. For example, the highest court in the nation, the U.S. Supreme Court, refused in 1985 to help a high school guidance counselor after she was fired for telling her secretary that she was in love with a woman. The Supreme Court refused even to hear the case.

Finally, lesbian and gay Americans can face more than the loss of a job. From verbal harassment to physical assault and murder, antigay violence touches lesbian and gay Americans in every part of the nation. In Michigan, thirty-two-year-old Scott Amedure died from two shotgun blasts after he appeared on a TV talk show and said he had a secret crush on a man. The man later confessed to killing Amedure. In Savannah, Georgia, three U.S. Army rangers were convicted of attacking and beating a gay man, thirty-three-year-old Wayne Lee, in a vacant lot. The doctor who admitted Lee to the hospital said that Lee was "probably the most mutilated person I have ever seen still alive."[10] In Bangor, Maine, three teenagers attacked twenty-three-year-old Charles Howard and a friend as they walked home from a church meeting. The teenagers yelled antigay names as they beat Howard. The teenagers then threw Howard off a bridge into a stream, where he drowned. Antilesbian violence turned a camping trip on the Appalachian Trial from a pleasant outing into horror for one lesbian couple. Rebecca Wight was shot to death, and her life partner, Claudia Brenner, was critically wounded by a man who stalked them and then ambushed them during a camp-out.

"I feel incredibly sad," Brenner says. "Sad that Rebecca is dead, sad that we were living our lives appropriately, honestly, innocently, and that someone hated who we were so much that he wanted us dead."[11]

Although all minorities are the target of hate crimes, crimes against homosexuals are increasing. Klanwatch, the investigative arm of the Southern Poverty Law Center in Montgomery, Alabama, reports that antigay bias accounted for 25 percent of all bias-related assaults and nearly two-thirds of all bias-related murders in 1994.[12]

A survey of thirty states and the District of Columbia reports 151 murders of lesbian and gay Americans in a two-year period in the 1990s. All of the crimes were hate crimes where the victim's sexual orientation was the focus of the rage. Almost 60 percent of the murders involved "overkill"— excessive force such as four or more gunshots or stab wounds or the repeated use of blunt objects. Arrests were reported in only 51 percent of the cases studied. This is much lower than the 66 percent national arrest rate for homicides.[13]

The study also found that violence against homosexuals increases when gay issues are in the news. For example, when the antigay proposal, Amendment 2, was passed in Colorado there was a wave of gay bashings. Antigay violence also shot up in New York City in 1994 during the twenty-fifth-anniversary commemoration of the Stonewall Rebellion and the Gay Games, a gathering of lesbian and gay athletes. During those events the rate of antigay violence was six times higher than the level of antigay violence in New York City during the previous year.[14]

When civil rights opponents increase their activity, antigay violence also increases. In a period of sixteen months when opponents became more vocal in Texas, eight gay men were murdered. One case in November 1993 involved Nicholus West, twenty-three, an employee of a medical records company. West was abducted, terrorized for hours, and shot nine times by three men. One of the men who were arrested for the crime later said he enjoyed the idea of what he called "fag bashing."

"It's not a stretch to say that the statements made and positions taken by the radical right have helped to create a climate of hatred against lesbians and gays," wrote *Houston Post* columnist Juan R. Palomo.[15]

A DAY IN THE LIFE OF LESBIAN AND GAY KANSAS

What do lesbians and gay men do with their time? Civil rights opponents claim that lesbians and gay men build their lives around parties, bars, sex, and drugs. Civil rights supporters say lesbians and gays live little differently than heterosexuals. Who is right? And what does a day in the life of a lesbian and gay community look like?

Take a look at lesbian and gay Kansas. Like every state in the nation, Kansas has several lesbian and gay communities. Many of the communities are in cities such as Wichita, Topeka, and Manhattan. Other lesbians and gays live on ranches and farms. Some live in small towns, which in Kansas can be as tiny as fifty people.

The Kansas town with the most well-known population of lesbians and gays is Lawrence. Located in the northeast corner of the state, the town of about 65,000 is the home of the University of Kansas. Lawrence is also the only city in Kansas with a law protecting people from discrimination based on sexual orientation. Passed in 1995 by the Lawrence City Commission, the future of the law is uncertain. Opponents are continuing a campaign to repeal it.

On the morning of Friday, October 6, 1995, however, the struggle for civil rights was not on the minds of most lesbians and gays in Lawrence.[16] Dawn was rainy and cold as alarms went off, mostly between 6:30 and 7:30 A.M.

Some people, like Margery, have to get up earlier. Her alarm goes off at 5:30 so she can get to her job as a certified nurse's aide by 7:00 A.M. She works with elderly patients with Alzheimer's Disease.

Life partners[17] Jill and Karla get up just before 6:00 A.M. They wake Linda, Jill's six-year-old daughter, and then eat a breakfast of Grape Nuts with a sprinkling of sugar. Jill drives to her job in a hospital in nearby Kansas City. Karla takes Linda to school and then heads to her own job as a health care provider in Lawrence.

Life partners Roger and Ty get to sleep until 9:00 A.M. Both being graduate students at the university, they don't have classes on Fridays. Roger is studying social work, while Ty is earning a doctorate in French literature.

John gets up just in time to go to work in the public education department of the university student health center. He skips breakfast and drinks a cup of coffee at his desk.

Harvey sleeps late. He retired this year after more than thirty years as a printer, but his retirement has been anything but restful. His one indulgence is sleeping in. Harvey's life partner, Curt, gets up early to drive to Topeka. Balding and middle-aged, Curt recently returned to school to get a master's degree in social work. As part of his program, he works at the Menninger Clinic in Topeka. On this Friday, their house is quiet. Both of Harvey's children are grown and live away from home. Curt's twelve-year-old son, Jack, is staying with his mother this week. Next week, Jack will be back with Curt and Harvey. Before leaving the house, Curt makes coffee so it will be ready when Harvey wakes up.

Grace also has two grown children, but she is far from retired. A psychotherapist, she teaches at a college in Kansas City and has a private practice of clients. Grace and her life partner, Harriet, have breakfast in bed. They drink coffee, eat toast and sausage, and chat. Harriet is a medical researcher at the university.

At work, Margery decides to take her patients to the local mall for their daily walk. The rain makes it unpleasant for them to walk outside. In the mall, they get chocolate at a candy store and sit down to enjoy it. Margery watches in amazement as one woman relaxes with the candy. This woman is normally frantic and anxious. Margery smiles as she watches the woman eat the chocolate slowly and calmly.

Roger and Ty treat themselves to a study break by visiting the Lawrence Public Library's annual used-book sale.

John sits at his computer for much of the day, working on improving the health center's new home page on the World Wide Web.

Harvey heads to work at the local antique mall where he and Curt sell the treasures they find at estate sales.

Grace spends most of her day on paperwork.

By 6:00 P.M. most of the lesbians and gays have left work. Margery has to stay an extra hour at work because a coworker calls in sick.

Jill and Karla pick up Linda and hurry to attend an open house and fund-raiser at the school where Linda is in the first grade. Jill's parents also attend. All of them chat with Linda's teacher. They see another lesbian couple there and say hello.

John and a friend drive to Kansas City to see the Andrew Wyeth exhibit at the Nelson-Atkins Art Museum. They dine afterwards on spaghetti at an inexpensive Kansas City restaurant.

Harvey's daughter and son-in-law stop at Harvey and Curt's house for a visit. The three of them chat until Curt comes home, then Harvey and Curt go to the movies and see *To Wong Foo With Love*—a Hollywood version of gay life.

Many of the Lawrence lesbians eventually make their way to the monthly lesbian potluck, which is held that night. Fried chicken, baked beans, cole slaw, tossed salad, banana nut bread, and green bean casserole made with mushroom soup are among the many dishes on the kitchen table. Apple cider, water, and cola are served for drinks. The dinner is held at a different lesbian's house each month. This month the house is small and on the poor side of town.

The routine for the dinner is always the same. Lesbians gather first to talk and eat. About an hour later, the hostess loudly proclaims that it is time for announcements. On this night, the house is crowded and noisy. The women take several minutes to quiet down, then lesbians stand to talk. They announce concerts and upcoming events. A couple volunteers to hold next month's potluck and announce their address. Several women talk about the building opposition to Lawrence's civil rights law.

When announcements are over, the women visit with each other. Public school teachers compare notes about problem students and talk about discipline. A recently graduated chemist who just moved to Lawrence is introduced to Harriet, the established scientist. The two chat about colleagues and research. A grandmother talks about her grandchildren.

In Kansas City, John and his friend get in their car for the drive home. They are best friends and not lovers. Because they are tired, they plan to part soon after arriving home in Lawrence.

Harvey and Curt arrive home from seeing *To Wong Foo*. They agree that it was mildly entertaining but wildly unrealistic. Unlike the characters in the movie, neither Harvey nor Curt dresses as women.

Roger and Ty visit with friends.

At the lesbian potluck, Margery says that she has to work on Saturday and she and her life partner leave. Grace and Harriet head home to spend a few quiet moments together. By 10:00 P.M., most of the women have left. After all the commotion, the house is quiet.

A WORLD WITHOUT HOMOSEXUALITY

At times it seems as if some people would prefer a world where no lesbians or gays existed. But what would that world really look like? Here is a look at what the world might have been like if it had never included people who were homosexual or had a significant homosexual experience in life.[18]

President Gerald Ford might have died in 1975 because gay ex-marine Oliver "Bill" Sipple would not have been alive to push away the gun of an assassin in San Francisco.

The United States, Britain, and the other Allies might have lost World War II because Alan Turing, a gay British mathematician, would never have been born. Turing broke one of the Nazis' most important codes to help shorten the war.

African-Americans might have struggled longer before receiving civil rights because there would have been no Bayard Rustin, the gay man who organized the 1963 March on Washington. This is the march where Dr. Martin Luther King, Jr., made his famous "I Have a Dream" speech.

Our musical world would have been impoverished because gay American composer Aaron Copeland would never have been born. Russian composer Peter Ilyich Tchaikovsky would not have existed, neither would have Leonard Bernstein, English composer Benjamin Britten, or singers Bessie Smith, Melissa Etheridge, or Elton John.

Western art would look very different because neither Michelangelo nor Leonardo da Vinci would have been born.

The hit Disney movies *The Little Mermaid and Beauty and the Beast* would have been much duller because Howard Ashman would not have been alive to write their Academy Award–winning songs.

Literature would have been impoverished because many authors would never have been born, including Pulitzer Prize–winning poet W. H. Auden, Nobel Prize–winning author Patrick White of Australia, E. M. Forster, Virginia Woolf, Willa Cather, Gertrude Stein, and Walt Whitman.

Movie theaters would have been duller: no Rock Hudson or Marlene Dietrich or Montgomery Clift. Actually, many of the most important plays of the American stage would never have been written because gay playwright Tennessee Williams would not have existed.

Who else would have been missing? The list of people who have had significant same-sex relationships is very long and includes Socrates, King Richard the Lion Hearted, and Queen Christina of Sweden.

QUESTIONS AND ANSWERS ABOUT SEXUAL ORIENTATION

From the American Psychological Association[19]

Is Sexual Orientation a Choice?

No. Sexual orientation emerges for most people in early adolescence without any prior sexual experience. And some people report trying very hard over many years to change their sexual orientation from homosexual to heterosexual with no success. For these reasons, psychologists do not consider sexual orientation for most people to be a conscious choice that can be changed voluntarily.

Is homosexuality a mental illness or emotional problem?

No. Psychologists, psychiatrists, and other mental health professionals agree that homosexuality is not an illness, mental disorder, or emotional problem. Much objective scientific research over the past thirty-five years shows us that homosexual orientation, in and of itself, is not associated with emotional or social problems.

Homosexuality was thought to be a mental illness in the past because mental health professionals and society had biased information about homosexuality since most studies involved only lesbians and gay men in therapy. When researchers examined data about gay people who were not in therapy, the idea that homosexuality was a mental illness was found to be untrue.

In 1973, the American Psychiatric Association confirmed the importance of the new research by removing the term *homosexuality* from the official manual that lists all mental and emotional disorders. In 1975, the American Psychological Association passed a resolution supporting this action. Both associations urge all mental health professionals to help dispel the stigma of mental illness that some people still associate with homosexual orientation. Since the original declassification of homosexuality as a mental disorder, this decision has subsequently been reaffirmed by additional research findings and both associations.

CHAPTER 3

BATTLEGROUND: RELIGION

THE ISSUES

1. Should homosexuality be considered a sin, a disease, or simply a difference that is neither good nor bad?

2. Should lesbians and gays be allowed to be members of a church?

3. Should lesbians and gays be allowed to marry in church?

4. Should lesbians and gays be ordained as clergy?

THE ARGUMENTS

Homosexuality is a sin. It must be condemned to keep it from spreading.

1. The Bible condemns homosexuality.

2. Any group of people that ignores the Bible will face the wrath of God. In fact, that is the point of the biblical story of the city of Sodom, which was destroyed by God because its inhabitants practiced homosexuality.

3. Homosexuality has been considered a sin by Christianity and Judaism for thousands of years.

4. Whether or not homosexuality has a biological cause, homosexuals must struggle against their impulses and learn to live as God intended. If homosexuals are unable to live a heterosexual life, then they must remain celibate. All humans are born into sin. That doesn't mean people should give in to it.

5. No matter how homosexuals live—no matter how monogamous or how loving or how religious—they are living in sin because heterosexuality is the only acceptable form of sexuality.

6. Supporters of civil rights for homosexuals are violating the religious rights of religious Americans.

Homosexuality is a difference that is morally neutral—neither good nor bad. What matters is how an individual lives, not whether he or she is homosexual or heterosexual.

1. Not all religions—not even all Christian churches—condemn homosexuality. Several denominations ordain lesbian and gay ministers and perform same-sex marriages.

2. Even among denominations whose leaders condemn homosexuality, many theologians, ministers, priests, and lay members disagree and argue for equality for lesbians and gays.

3. Scholars are divided on the question of whether the Bible actually condemns homosexuality or whether the antigay statements are inaccurate translations.

4. Basing public policy on an interpretation of the Bible is dangerous because the Bible has often been used to justify prejudice and discrimination.

5. Antigay groups are attempting to impose their religious beliefs on all Americans and to deny people their fundamental right to freedom of religion.

6. Religious leaders and religious groups that preach intolerance are contributing to the wave of violence faced by lesbian and gay Americans.

In many ways, religion has been the most important battleground in the fight over civil rights. Opponents often base their opposition on religious arguments, declaring that homosexuality is a sin that is helping to cause "America's moral decline."[1] In debates on city commissions and in state legislatures, conservative clergy and their churches often lead the opponents of lesbians and gays.

On the national level, the leading opposition groups are religious-based organizations such as the Christian Coalition and the Traditional Values Coalition. The Christian Coalition, for example, has supporters in 60,000 churches around the country. The churches not only provide recruits for the Christian Coalition, but they also act as local headquarters for the coalition's work. On the third Tuesday of every month, people meet in more than two hundred churches around the nation and watch a satellite broadcast from the Christian Coalition's national headquarters. The broadcast relays the coalition's monthly instructions on political organizing.[2]

Religion is also a battleground in the sense that many churches are arguing within themselves about their stand on lesbian and gay Americans. Among the many denominations engaged in heated debate on the subject are Episcopalians, Lutherans, Methodists, and Presbyterians. Beginning in the 1980s, each of those denominations has had at least one major fight over the issue. Episcopal bishop John Shelby Spong of Newark, New Jersey, for example, has ordained openly gay priests and argued for homosexuality to be declared "morally neutral" by his church, while other Episcopal leaders angrily oppose his view. Special committees of the United Methodist and Presbyterian churches have studied the issue and recommended that both denominations ordain lesbians and gays, but leaders of these churches rejected their recommendations. Meanwhile, people on both sides of the debate have vowed to continue to fight.[3]

THE EVIDENCE

Religious Attitudes About Homosexuality

Although civil rights opponents often argue that all religions oppose homosexuality, there is no one religious position on the topic. Views vary even within Christianity, which has produced most of the leaders of the antigay opposition. Opinions range from that of Reverend Fred Phelps, a Baptist preacher in Kansas who believes homosexuals should be executed, to the United Church of Christ which ordains lesbian and gay ministers.

The attitudes of Christian denominations are particularly important to understand because of the leading role Christian ministers have taken in the civil rights opposition. Within Christianity, attitudes toward homosexuality generally fall into three categories:[4]

> **1. Homosexuality is sinful and unnatural, and homosexuals are lost souls.** Sexual intimacy between people of the same sex is viewed as immoral, unnatural, and degrading to human dignity. Any society that condones homosexuality will be punished by God. Some people who have this view argue that homosexuality is a choice. Others say that sexual orientation is biologically determined. All agree that the only way for homosexuals to live morally is to either change to heterosexuality or be celibate and live without being sexually active. People with this position usually oppose civil rights laws.

57

2. Homosexuality is essentially imperfect, but homosexuals are not lost. This view suggests a middle ground. Homosexuals are not seen as being responsible for their condition, and are not condemned. Because all humans are sinners, homosexuals must not be driven from the Church. Homosexual unions are preferable to promiscuity, but heterosexual marriage is still the ideal. People with this position may support civil rights laws at the same time that they oppose same-sex marriages and the ordination of lesbians and gays.

3. Homosexuality is natural. As such, it is neither good nor bad. This view suggests that sexual orientation is morally neutral. Under this view the sins of sexuality are not same-sex relationships, but selfishness, promiscuity, and the use of coercion by both heterosexuals and homosexuals. Biblical condemnations of homosexuality are seen as being based on inaccurate translations. Sometimes people say that the translations are accurate but must be placed in the context of history. These people argue that condemnations of homosexuality should be discarded like other outdated concepts such as biblical support for slavery. People with this position support civil rights for lesbians and gays, the ordination of homosexual clergy, and same-sex marriages.

Other religions, such as Judaism and Islam, are no more unified in their position on homosexuality than Christianity. The attitudes of American Jews generally fall into the same three categories found in Christianity. Islam, on the whole, has been more tolerant than Christianity. While fundamentalists have often condemned homosexuality and punished lesbians and gays, other followers of Islam have been tolerant and supportive.

When civil rights opponents argue that all religions condemn homosexuality, they are also ignoring the fact that many members of their own denominations disagree with them. Because dissenters face expulsion from their denomination if their attitudes are known, progay clergy and churches often remain hidden. This makes it impossible to judge the number of dissenters, but they obviously do exist. Even the fervently antigay Baptists have dissenters, with two churches in North Carolina providing such strong support of homosexuals in the early 1990s that they performed marriage ceremonies for same-sex couples.

Another strong opponent of homosexuals, the Roman Catholic Church, also has dissenters. As early as 1975, a committee of Catholic theologians called the American Theological Society's Committee on Sexuality released a report declaring that homosexuality is a "natural and irreversible state." In 1976, the Young Adult Ministry Board of the U.S. Catholic Conference voted to support lesbians and gays, declaring that homosexuals suffer from "questionable scriptural interpretation." A task force of the San Francisco Archdiocese of the Roman Catholic Church made fifty-four progay recommendations in a report issued in 1982, calling for an end to antigay violence and for recognition of the spiritual value of lesbian and gay sexuality.[5]

The Bible and Homosexuality

Civil rights opponents often justify their opposition by quoting the Bible. Three sections are often quoted—the story of the destruction of the city of Sodom, the priestly codes of Leviticus, and the letters of Paul.

The most well known is the tale of Sodom, which has become so identified with homosexuality that laws banning same-sex behavior are called sodomy laws. In the antigay interpretation of the story, God destroyed the city of Sodom with sulfur and fire because its inhabitants were homosexuals. Many modern biblical scholars, however, disagree.[6] Instead, they argue that the true sin of Sodom was inhospitality.

The story recounted in Genesis 19:4–11 starts when two angels arrive in the town of Sodom and meet Lot, who invites them into his home and feeds them a meal. The men of Sodom then surround Lot's house and demand that Lot surrender the two visitors so "that we may know them." Lot offers his two virgin daughters to the crowd instead. He and his daughters are finally rescued by the angels. Civil rights opponents argue that the men in the crowd wanted to rape the male angels. Many modern biblical scholars, however, say this is an inaccurate translation of the original Hebrew. Scholars also note that opponents ignore the fact that most biblical references to Sodom describe the city's sins as selfishness, arrogance, and inhospitality. (See Isaiah 1, Jeremiah 23, and Jesus' words in Luke 10:10–12). The prophet Ezekiel says in Ezekiel 16:49:

> This was the guilt of your sister Sodom: she and her
> daughters had pride, excess of food, and prosperous ease,
> but did not aid the poor and needy.

To a modern reader, the sin of inhospitality may not seem to deserve the destruction of a city. However, the two angels came to Sodom in a era when travel was dangerous. There were no fast-food rest stops on the dusty trails that served as roads. A traveler's survival depended on hospitality. By being inhospitable, the men of Sodom might well have condemned the two strangers to death.

Reverend Edward Bowman, a United Methodist pastor, is one of many clergy who denounce the use of the story of Sodom to condemn homosexuals. "The real irony is that homosexuals have been the victim of inhospitality for thousands of years in the Christian nations of the world," Bowman says. "Condemned by the church and the state, they have been ridiculed, rejected, persecuted, and even executed. In the name of an erroneous interpretation of the crime of Sodom, the true crime of Sodom has been continuously perpetrated to our own day."[7]

The second biblical reference that is often used to denounce lesbians and gays is found in Leviticus in the following verses:

> You shall not lie with a man as with a woman; it is an abomination. (Leviticus 18:22)

> If a man lies with a male as with a woman, both of them have committed an abomination; they shall be put to death; their blood is upon them. (Leviticus 20:13)

Scholars say that these references must be understood in context. These laws are included in a long list of other Old Testament laws that are routinely ignored today. These include laws forbidding the consumption of shellfish, planting two kinds of crops in the same field, and generally forbidding the combination of two different things.

Methodist writer Bruce Hilton argues that these laws have become irrelevant. "Taking the priestly codes literally in the twentieth century raises some real problems," Hilton says. "We don't feel condemned for wearing a shirt of 65 percent cotton and 35 percent Dacron, because that prohibition spoke well but specifically to a situation no longer meaningful. We still deplore adultery, or cursing one's parents. But we don't apply the Levites' prescribed punishment: death by stoning. If we try to apply these rules literally, it seems to me we must apply them all, not picking and choosing. And taking them literally puts us in conflict with the teaching far more basic to our faith—that the old law was replaced with the new grace in the coming of Jesus Christ."[8]

Civil rights opponents also quote the letters of Paul in the New Testament. Those references are:

> For this cause God gave them up until vile affections; for even their women did change the natural use into that which is against nature. (Romans 1:26)

> And likewise also the men, leaving the natural use of the women, burned in their lust one toward another, men with men working that which is unseemly, and receiving in themselves that recompense of their error which was meet. (Romans 1:27)

> Know ye not that the unrighteous shall not inherit the kingdom of God? Be not deceived; neither fornicators, nor idolaters, nor adulterers, nor effeminate, nor abusers of themselves with mankind. (I Corinthians 6:9)

Biblical scholars say there are many problems with interpreting these passages as a ban on homosexuality. One key problem involves differences in translation. Depending on the version of the Bible quoted, for example, the passage from Corinthians can mean eight different things, including several interpretations that do not involve homosexuality.

Scholars also argue that these passages condemn practices as being homosexual that no longer exist. These practices include temple prostitution. Most importantly, scholars and ministers argue that none of these verses refer to homosexuality as it is known today. The modern concept of homosexuality was not even known until the nineteenth century. All the biblical references to homosexuality assume that the people engaging in same-sex acts are heterosexuals who are acting in a way contrary to their nature.

"Let's face it," Reverend Fred Pattison says."The Old Covenant religious leader, the priest of the Hebrews, could not possibly conceive of healthy normal, God-centered same-sex relationships—why? These priests had only been exposed to same-sex acts as practiced by their pagan neighbors and that always in association with idolatrous religious worship.

"To the Jews, and to us as well, such practices were blasphemy. To the Jews, homosexual sexual practices were always associated with temple prostitution and that in extremely perverted forms; hence the only conclusion that could be arrived at was that all homosexuality was evil, false, pagan, and against nature and God!"[9]

Finally, many ministers argue that Christians, at least, should remember that Jesus never condemned homosexuality. None of the Gospels report that Jesus ever said anything on the subject. Hilton suggests that Jesus may have had an opinion about homosexuality, but that it is "fair to suggest" that neither he nor the men who wrote the Bible considered it a major concern.

"When Jesus condemned human behavior, it was likely to be self-righteousness and arrogance," Hilton says. "If he never mentioned homosexual acts, he certainly spoke often of the hardness of heart of religious insiders. He clearly wished religious institutions would leave the business of judging to God."[10]

The Bible and Public Policy

Many people today believe that using the Bible as a basis for writing laws is a dangerous practice. They say they are concerned because the Bible has often been used to support prejudice and discrimination. In fact, the Bible was once used to support both slavery and segregation. Biblical scholars argue that the way racists used the Bible was remarkably similar to the way civil rights opponents use it against lesbians and gays today. At one time, slave owners even labeled slavery a "divine institution."[11]

Although biblically based racist writings date from the earliest days of the American colonies, the largest number of works date from the period just before the Civil War. Those books include Josiah Priest's *Bible Defense of Slavery: Origin, Fortunes and History of the Negro Race*, published in 1852; Howell Cobb's *A Scriptural Examination of the Institution of Slavery in the United States*, published in 1856; and David Ewart's *A Scriptural View of the Moral Relations of African Slavery*, published in 1859.

In these books, the writers argued that the Bible clearly showed God's support for slavery. As proof, they cited the many examples of slavery in the Old Testament and cited the instructions regarding behavior of slaves and masters in the New Testament. Among other things, these verses say that slaves should be obedient and subservient (Titus 2:9–10; Ephesians 6:5–9; Colossians 3:22–25; and I Peter 2:18–25), slaves should have regard for their master (I Timothy 6:1–2; Ephesians 6:5–9), runaway slaves should be returned (Philemon), and that God intended for there to be many different levels of human status (I Corinthians 12:13–26).

Underlying all of the American proslavery arguments was the belief that scripture declared that Africans were morally inferior and had been cursed by God. Much as antigay groups today use the biblical story of Sodom against lesbians and gays, proslavery forces used the story of Ham to justify their actions.[12] To these writers, the story was proof that "African slavery is a punishment, inflicted upon the enslaved, for their wickedness."[13]

In the twentieth-century fight over African-American civil rights in the South, white racists continued to use the Bible to justify segregation laws. Baptists in Arkansas even resolved that the races must be kept apart because "God in His divine wisdom ordained that man should maintain a pure blood stream in his own race."[14]

The Separation of Church and State

Despite the fact that religion plays a key role in the antigay movement, in one sense any mention of religion is irrelevant in the debate over civil rights. This is because the U.S. Constitution demands the separation of church and state. Separation of church and state means that the government can neither impose a state-sponsored religion nor allow any church or religious sect to force its ideas on people who are not church members.[15]

Although many of them were deeply religious, the men who wrote the Constitution firmly believed that government must be kept separate from religion. That is because they had seen firsthand what can happen when government and church become one. Many colonists fled Europe to escape the restrictions that governments put on their religious lives. When they arrived in the Americas, many again suffered under religious persecution, only this time it came from colonial governments. There are numerous examples. The Puritans set up the Massachusetts Bay colony as a theocratic (religiously based) state. In that state, Catholics, Quakers, and the followers of other minority religions were punished by death. Catholics, in turn, fled the repression of Massachusetts and founded another colony in Maryland, where they persecuted Protestants and even some Catholics who worshipped in nontraditional ways.[16]

Today many of the strongest supporters of the separation of church and state are ministers. The North American Division of Seventh-Day Adventists, for example, publishes a magazine called *Liberty*, which is dedicated to discussion of religious freedom. The magazine's Declaration of Principles notes that "the God-given right of religious liberty is best exercised when church and state are separate."[17]

Reverend W. W. Finlater, the pastor of the Pullen Memorial Baptist Church in Raleigh, North Carolina, agrees. Finlater says the principle of separation of church and state "guarantees that the government will not take sides—and that each of us will be free to practice and teach our religion according to our individual consciences."[18]

THE RELIGIOUS LIFE OF LESBIANS AND GAYS

Although lesbian and gay Americans are often stereotyped as rejecting religion, the reality is far different. In fact, while religions have sometimes rejected them, lesbians and gays have embraced spirituality. The extent of religious activity in gay and lesbian America can be glimpsed by logging on to the spirituality message board on America Online's Gay and Lesbian Community Forum. In the first nine months of its existence, more than 3,000 messages were posted by lesbians and gays identifying themselves, among other things, as Baptists, Mormons, Seventh-Day Adventists, Catholics, Episcopalians, Lutherans, Presbyterians, Jehovah's Witnesses, Baha'i, and Buddhists. In their messages, they discussed theology, their experience in their churches, and where to find gay-friendly congregations. Sometimes, they just offered support for one another.

Because many churches are hostile to homosexuals, lesbians and gays have had to find many different ways to make religion a part of their lives. Some lesbian and gay ministers have openly announced their sexual orientation to their congregations and then lost their churches. Some lesbian and gay lay members have also been forced out of their congregations when people knew they were homosexual. To continue their worship, they and other lesbians and gays have formed support groups. Groups such as Dignity (Catholic), Integrity (Episcopalian), and Acceptance (Methodist) have given a spiritual home to many lesbians and gays. Other groups, such as Evangelicals Concerned, have provided Bible-study groups and worship for lesbian and gay Christian fundamentalists.

Other lesbians and gays left their own churches and joined the Universal Fellowship of Metropolitan Community Churches. The denomination is based in Los Angeles and has churches in many cities, including Paducah, Kentucky, Topeka, Kansas, and Fort Lauderdale, Florida. The denomination's largest congregation is in Dallas, Texas. More than 1,400 people, including a minority of heterosexuals, attend the two Sunday services at the Cathedral of Hope. The 34,000-square-foot, $3.5 million church was built in 1993. Members of the congregation say the church plays an indispensable role in their lives.

"The Cathedral of Hope is such a wonderful name because so many of us were without hope," said David Pfleeger, forty-one, who grew up attending a conservative church in Tulsa, Oklahoma. "Sometimes openly and sometimes not so openly, we were told Jesus didn't love us anymore."[19]

CHAPTER 4

BATTLEGROUND: DECRIMINALIZING HOMOSEXUALITY

THE ISSUE

Should homosexuality be decriminalized? In other words, should consenting adults of the same sex be allowed to have intimate relations in their own homes?

THE ARGUMENTS

Laws making homosexuality illegal should remain on the books.

1. The Bible condemns homosexuality, therefore the full force of the law should be used to repress it. Any group of people that ignores the Bible will face the wrath of God.
2. Homosexuality is not a "victimless" crime. The victims are homosexuals who lead miserable sex-addicted lives and the innocent children who are molested by homosexuals.
3. If homosexuality is illegal, then homosexuals might be forced to seek treatment.
4. Legalizing homosexuality condones homosexuality and sends a message to young people that they should consider this a lifestyle choice. This threatens the family and will ultimately destroy American society.

5. The highest court of the land supported these laws in *Bowers v. Hardwick*.

These laws should be repealed.

1. Not all religions—not even all Christians—condemn homosexuality. By using a religious argument, antigay groups are also attempting to impose their religious beliefs on other Americans.

2. The reality of homosexual life is far different from the stereotypes people use to justify these laws. The picture of the homosexual as a miserable, sex-addicted pervert is a stereotype based on prejudice—not on factual information.

3. Because they usually target homosexuals and ignore heterosexuals, these laws violate the right to equal protection under the law as guaranteed by the Fifth and Fourteenth Amendments to the Constitution. These laws also violate the right to privacy (the right to be left alone), as guaranteed by the Fourth, Fifth, Ninth, and Fourteenth Amendments and upheld by a series of Supreme Court rulings.

4. Allowing homosexuals to live free of fear of arrest and harassment will not turn heterosexuals gay, nor will it undermine heterosexual families.

5. The Supreme Court decision did not make it illegal to repeal these laws.

6. The Supreme Court is as wrong on this issue as it was when it upheld the constitutionality of slavery and racial segregation. Someday the Court will reverse itself on this issue just as it reversed those other decisions.

Today, homosexuality is outlawed in almost half of the United States. Lesbian and gay citizens risk arrest, fines, or jail for having intimate sexual relations in the privacy of their own homes. Even same-sex couples who have been married in church services can be arrested and convicted of breaking the law. Penalties range from a two-hundred-dollar fine to twenty years in prison. Known as sodomy laws, these statutes make it a criminal offense to engage in certain sexual activities. Although the laws vary from state to state, most often they make it illegal to engage in activities such as oral sex and anal intercourse. In some states, sodomy laws also make it illegal for heterosexuals to engage in these activities, although the laws are not enforced against heterosexuals.

In fact, sodomy laws are rarely even enforced against homosexuals, but the laws remain important to the debate over civil rights. In the places where they are still on the books, sodomy laws justify attacks on lesbians and gay men. By making their most private activities illegal, sodomy laws send the message that lesbians and gays are outlaws and that government, society, and individuals are justified in discriminating against them. Sodomy laws have also been used as a justification for denying lesbians and gays custody of their children, banning books from libraries, and denying civil rights protection.

The first major effort to decriminalize homosexuality came from a group of legal scholars, judges, and lawyers called the American Law Institute. In the mid-1950s, the institute drafted a model criminal code. Among many other things, the code suggested repealing laws that prohibited sexual behavior between consenting adults, including sodomy laws.

When the institute began its campaign to convince states to pass the model code, every state in the nation had a sodomy law. In 1961, Illinois became the first state to repeal its sodomy law by adopting the code. Another twenty-seven other states would eventually repeal the laws. The campaign, however, eventually ground to a halt in the 1980s as civil rights opponents grew stronger politically. The last state to repeal a sodomy law was Wisconsin, which did it in 1983.

In 1986, civil rights supporters thought they had finally won their fight to legalize homosexuality when the U.S. Supreme Court agreed to decide a case on the issue. Known as *Bowers v. Hardwick*, the case involved Michael Hardwick, a gay man who was arrested in Atlanta in 1981 for having sex with another man in his own bedroom. The arrest occurred when a visiting friend who had been sleeping on Hardwick's couch was awakened by a knock on the door. Not knowing that Hardwick and his lover were in the bedroom, the visiting friend let a police officer into Hardwick's apartment. The police officer went to Hardwick's bedroom door and looked in.

"I heard [a] noise and I looked up, and this officer is standing in my bedroom," Hardwick says. "He identified himself when he realized I had seen him. He said, 'My name is Officer Torick. Michael Hardwick, you are under arrest.' I said, 'For what? What are you doing in my bedroom?'"[1]

Hardwick and his lover were arrested and spent twelve hours in jail. Despite the fact that the Georgia sodomy law carries a penalty of up to twenty years in prison, the charges were later dropped. Hardwick decided to challenge the sodomy law, however, and filed a federal lawsuit protesting his arrest. One federal court declared the sodomy law to be unconstitutional, but the Supreme Court disagreed and voted 5-4 to declare that the law is constitutional.

71

Religion as an Argument for Sodomy Laws

When civil rights opponents use religion as a basis for their arguments, they are stepping outside of the Constitution. U.S. Supreme Court justice Harry Blackmun made this point in his dissenting opinion in *Bowers v. Hardwick*.

"That certain, but by no means all, religious groups condemn the behavior at issue gives the state no license to impose their judgments on the entire citizenry," Blackmun wrote.[2]

See Chapter 3 for a discussion of the separation of church and state.

The Reality of Lesbian and Gay Life

Civil rights opponents also argue that sodomy laws must be retained because they believe homosexuality hurts people, and that homosexuals are sexual criminals who molest children. Scientists report, however, that research does not support this belief.

The reality of lesbian and gay life is far different from that portrayed by the opponents of civil rights. No major psychiatric, psychological, or medical association recognizes homosexuality as an illness. More than twenty years of research has also found that there is no such thing as one kind of homosexual personality, including a personality that molests children. There is also no scientific evidence indicating that homosexuals as a group are more neurotic, unhappy, or psychologically ill than heterosexuals. In fact, scientific studies suggest that the only way to portray homosexuality as a crime, particularly as a crime that hurts people, is to ignore scientific research and take stereotype, myth, and propaganda as fact.[3] For a more detailed discussion of lesbian and gay life, see Chapter 2.

Perhaps the most dangerous stereotype is the one that portrays lesbians and gays as child molesters. This stereotype is particularly dangerous for children because it ignores the fact that most child molesters are heterosexual. One study found that children were more than one hundred times as likely to be molested by a heterosexual than a homosexual.

The study was led by Dr. Carole Jenny, head of the child advocacy and protection team at the University of Colorado Health Sciences Center and Children's Hospital in Denver. Her team of researchers reviewed nearly three hundred cases of child abuse reported to the hospital's sexual abuse clinic from July 1, 1991, to June 30, 1992. Every case treated by the clinic was reviewed. Of the 269 cases that involved an adult molesting a child, the researchers discovered only two offenders who were homosexual. In 82 percent of the cases, the alleged offender was a heterosexual partner of a close relative of the child.[4]

"We see a few cases where a predatory gay male or a predatory lesbian woman molests the kids, but it's very rare," Jenny told newspaper reporters. "The idea that there are legions of people out there preying on small children—well, most of those folks are in their families."[5]

A. Nicholas Groth, a leading researcher on sexual assault, says that the belief that lesbians and gays are particularly attracted to children is "completely unsupported" by his research.[6]

Groth and Jean Birnbaum published a groundbreaking study of Massachusetts sex offenders in 1978. In their study, they found that 76 percent of the child molesters were exclusively heterosexual, while 24 percent could be classified as bisexual, which means they are attracted to both women and men. Even the bisexual men preferred female sexual partners to male partners. When the bisexual men did molest boys, they did so because boys were more readily available than girls. Groth and Birnbaum believe that homosexuality and child molesting may be "mutually exclusive." Heterosexual males often molest boys because their youth makes them appear more feminine than masculine, which would be a turn-off to gay men, the researchers say.[7] Since the 1978 study was published, Groth says he has worked with another 3,000 child molesters. None of those experiences has led him to doubt the findings of his original study, Groth says.

Many people argue that the myth of the homosexual child molester is very dangerous and not just to homosexuals. *The Oregonian* newspaper of Portland, Oregon, argues:

> *The danger of parents linking the two [homosexuality and child molesting] is that they may be so watchful for signs of sexual abuse by a homosexual counselor or teacher that they miss the more likely candidates—their own relatives, family friends or neighbors. If children are led to believe that homosexuals or some other scary people "out there" are the ones they should fear, they won't be prepared to deal with attempted abuse by someone who does not fit that profile.*[8]

Homosexuality and the Heterosexual Family

Civil rights opponents argue that sodomy laws are important because they keep homosexuality from spreading and thus keep it from threatening the heterosexual family. Scientists again report, however, that this argument is based on a myth. Researchers who study families say that the real dangers facing heterosexual families have nothing to do with homosexuality, but with other factors.

A divorce rate of 50 percent, alcoholism, drug abuse, poverty, unemployment, wife battering, child abuse, child neglect, and absent parents who refuse to pay child support are among the many real dangers that face the heterosexual family today. Even some conservative Christians agree with the researchers. Evangelist and author Tony Campolo argues that "divorce, not gays and lesbians, is what will destroy the American family."

"Christians are quick to condemn drugs, crime, and homosexuality, but slow to acknowledge their own shortcomings," he says. "Pious, insensitive attitudes concerning issues like poverty and discrimination are contributing to the overall decline of the family."[9]

A Closer Look at the *Bowers v. Hardwick* Decision

It might seem like the fight over sodomy laws ended with the Supreme Court's decision in the *Bowers v. Hardwick* case. Legal scholars, however, say the fight is far from over. The Supreme Court decision did not prohibit state legislatures from voting to repeal the laws. Furthermore, the decision only dealt with the U.S. Constitution. It did not prohibit individual state courts from ruling that sodomy laws violate state constitutions. Since *Bowers v. Hardwick* was decided, high courts in Michigan, Kentucky, and Texas have overturned sodomy laws in those states.

The future actions of the U.S. Supreme Court are also uncertain. The Court can reverse itself on the constitutionality of sodomy laws just as it once reversed itself on the constitutionality of slavery. In fact in *Bowers v. Hardwick*, the Supreme Court came very close to issuing a very different decision. The decision came on a split 5-4 vote. A change of one vote would have made the difference.

Journalists now report that the vote was almost different. In a preliminary meeting of justices on the case, Justice Lewis F. Powell first said he would vote to overturn Georgia's sodomy law. Several days after the meeting, Powell sent a memo to his fellow justices saying that he was switching his vote.[10] After he retired from the Supreme Court, Powell said he later realized that he had been wrong to change his vote.

"I think I probably made a mistake in that one," Powell said.

The case had been a "close call," Powell said, noting that his vote was based on the fact that the sodomy law had not been enforced for decades.[11]

Among the strongest opponents of sodomy laws were the four Supreme Court justices who were in the minority in the *Bowers v. Hardwick* case. Justices Blackmun, John P. Stevens, William J. Brennan and Thurgood Marshall all voted to overturn the laws.[12] In their written opinions, the four justices were replying to the majority opinions, which were written by Justice Byron White and Chief Justice Warren Burger.[13] White and Burger argued that lesbians and gays did not have a right to privacy because homosexuality had been outlawed for centuries. Homosexuals did not deserve the same treatment as heterosexuals because "no connection" has been proven between homosexuality and "family, marriage or procreation," White said.

In an angry dissenting opinion, Justice Blackmun said the majority had misread the Constitution and based their decision on intolerance. Blackmun quoted the late U.S. Supreme Court justice Oliver Wendell Holmes, who said that it is "revolting to have no better reason for a rule of law than that it was laid down in the time of Henry IV."

Blackmun added that it is wrong to condemn a way of life simply because it is different. *Bowers v. Hardwick* is about the right to be let alone, Blackmun said. In deciding as they did, the five justices set a dangerous precedent that could hurt heterosexuals as well as homosexuals.

"What the Court really has refused to recognize is the fundamental interest all individuals have in controlling the nature of their intimate associations with others," Blackmun wrote. The "heart of the Constitution's protection of privacy" is the right of an individual to have sexual relationships "in the intimacy of his or her own home."

In a separate opinion, Stevens, Brennan, and Marshall argued that the sodomy laws must be struck down because they violate the Constitution's most basic principle—the principle that "all men are created equal."

Blackmun ended his opinion by writing about his hope:

"I can only hope that . . . the Court soon will reconsider its analysis and conclude that depriving individuals of the right to choose for themselves how to conduct their intimate relationships poses a far greater threat to the values most deeply rooted in our Nation's history than tolerance of nonconformity could ever do."[13]

WHERE LESBIANS AND GAYS ARE CRIMINALS

Twenty states have laws that make it illegal for consenting adults of the same sex to have intimate sexual relations in the privacy of their homes. Those states are:

Alabama	Kansas	Oklahoma
Arizona	Louisiana	Rhode Island
Arkansas	Massachusetts	South Carolina
Delaware	Mississippi	Texas
Florida	Missouri	Utah
Georgia	Montana	Virginia
Idaho	North Carolina	

PORTRAIT OF A CHILD MOLESTER

Adults who sexually molest children are a diverse group. No one race, religion, level of intelligence, level of education, occupation, group of occupations, or income sets perpetrators apart from the rest of the population. So far, researchers and health care workers who treat molested children have found only a few characteristics shared by most—but not all—child molesters. Most often, child molesters are:

- heterosexual
- male
- acquainted with the victim.[14]

One study reported that a child's risk of being molested by a heterosexual is more than one hundred times greater than the chance of being molested by a lesbian or gay man. Many other studies have found that even when a same-sex assault occurs, the perpetrator is most often an individual who identifies himself as heterosexual and has adult heterosexual relationships. Some researchers have suggested that some heterosexual men molest boys because they are more accessible than girls. Being more adventurous, boys may be easier to lure into dangerous situations.

So far, studies have confirmed overwhelmingly that most child molesters are male. Among reported perpetrators, 90 percent or more are male. One national study found that as much as 17 percent of the male population acknowledged having molested a child. Some researchers have suggested, however, that more women may be perpetrators than are reported. Women's roles in child care may make it easier for them to hide the incidents of abuse.

Perhaps the most surprising finding of the past two decades of research is that the greatest danger children face is not from strangers.

"The child is at greatest risk inside the home," says Ernie Allen, president of the National Center for Missing and Exploited Children.[15]

One study found that out of the 139,000 confirmed cases of child sexual abuse reported to state child-protective service agencies in 1992, most of the children were thought to have been molested by relatives and friends. Another researcher studied adult women who reported being molested as children. Only 25 percent reported being abused by a stranger, while the rest reported being abused by relatives, family friends, neighbors, and authority figures like baby-sitters. A similar study of male victims found 34 percent were abused by strangers while the other 66 percent reported being abused by relatives and acquaintances.

Researchers have also found the stereotype of the "dirty old man" who molests children to be nothing more than a myth. One researcher found that all the perpetrators studied committed their first sexual offense with a child before age forty and 80 percent of the perpetrators committed their first offense before age thirty.

CHAPTER 5

BATTLEGROUND: PROTECTION FROM DISCRIMINATION

THE ISSUES

1. Should an employer have the right to refuse to hire people or to fire them because they are lesbian or gay?
2. Should a landlord be allowed to refuse to rent a house or apartment because the potential tenant is lesbian or gay?
3. Should a restaurant or a hotel have a right to refuse service to lesbians or gays, no matter how they act?
4. Is it constitutional for a city or state to forbid lesbians and gays from trying to pass antidiscrimination laws?

THE ARGUMENTS

Homosexuals should be denied protection.

1. Homosexuality is a lifestyle, not a minority. Homosexuality is not an unchangeable characteristic like skin color. Therefore, it does not deserve any kind of protection.
2. Like all Americans, homosexuals are protected by the Constitution and the Bill of Rights. Why do they need more laws?
3. In the *Bowers v. Hardwick* decision, the U.S. Supreme Court already said that homosexuals must be

treated differently than other Americans and denied the same rights.

4. Society has a compelling reason to discriminate against homosexuals. Homosexuality is an evil that must be stopped. Civil rights laws would put the stamp of approval on this horrible behavior.

5. Homosexuals want special rights. They want to use civil rights laws to impose their beliefs on others and to rob people of their freedom of religion. Civil rights laws would even keep parents from teaching values to their children.

6. Extending civil rights to homosexuals is a ridiculous idea that has little support in society.

Homosexuals should have civil rights protection.

1. Lesbians and gays suffer discrimination in all aspects of their lives.

2. Lesbians and gays have no protection under the Constitution and are seeking nothing more and nothing less than equal rights.

3. Nothing in the *Bowers v. Hardwick* decision prohibits a city council, state legislature, or the U.S. Congress from passing laws protecting lesbian and gay citizens from discrimination.

4. Neither the states nor the federal government has any interest in allowing discrimination to continue against lesbian and gay citizens. The arguments of opponents are based on myth, stereotypes, and prejudice.

5. Protecting the rights of lesbians and gays does not interfere with what parents do at home or what congregations do in church.

6. Proposals such as those passed in Colorado and Cincinnati deny millions of American citizens equal protection under the law and deny them access to the political process. These proposals also threaten all minorities.

7. Civil rights protection for lesbians and gays is supported by many people and organizations.

THE SITUATION

In the twentieth century, the power of the majority to discriminate against the minority has undergone a fundamental change. Once businesses and governments were free to discriminate against American citizens in almost any way they wished. Businesses, for example, could once hire people or fire them for any reason—whether or not the reason was related to performance on the job. At the same time, women and minorities had no way to fight back. The laws of the day did not allow people who were treated unfairly to sue in court. There were no public agencies to take complaints about discrimination. There were no penalties for anyone who discriminated against anyone else.

All of that changed because of the efforts of African-Americans, other minorities, and the women's rights movement. From the 1950s through the 1980s, the U.S. Supreme Court issued a series of rulings that made such unfair practices illegal. Beginning in 1964 with the Civil Rights Act, the U.S. Congress passed a series of laws to protect minorities and women from discrimination. Meanwhile, states, cities, and counties passed similar laws. States created civil rights commissions to hear complaints. The federal government established several different agencies to look into complaints and guarantee that all people really are treated equally.

Today, discrimination based on race, ethnicity, age, handicap, gender, or religion is illegal. For the first time, Americans who were unfairly kept out of a job, denied housing, or denied service in a public place can get help. Landlords and employers can be sued or complaints can be filed with a government agency. If an individual can prove that he or she has been treated unfairly, then the courts or a government agency can help. For example, an employment discrimination case might be resolved by making a guilty business pay a financial settlement to an employee who was treated unfairly.

Since the 1970s, lesbian and gay Americans and their heterosexual supporters have been campaigning to pass similar laws to guard against discrimination based on sexual orientation. These laws would protect heterosexuals as well as homosexuals. So far, nine states and more than one hundred cities and counties have passed these kinds of laws. A bill granting some form of civil rights protection for lesbians and gays has also been introduced every year in the U.S. Congress since Representative Bella Abzug (D–New York) first did it in 1975. The federal bill, however, has never come close to passing.

Despite early successes for lesbians and gays, the debate over antidiscrimination laws changed in the 1990s. Beginning with the 1992 election, civil rights opponents launched campaigns to prohibit government from providing legal protection based on sexual orientation. Sometimes, the proposals would have also made it illegal for government employees to provide any kind of support for lesbian and gay citizens or to even say anything positive about them. This means, among other things, that a teacher could not tell a high school English class that writer Willa Cather was a lesbian; it also means that lesbian and gay college students would not be allowed to form a club to meet on their campus. Some legal scholars believed that the proposals might have even kept a hospital from providing treatment to homosexuals.

These proposals appeared on the ballot in many states, including Washington, Oregon, Idaho, Colorado, Texas, Florida, Ohio, New Hampshire, and Maine. Although frequently defeated by voters, the proposals were approved in Colorado, Cincinnati, several cities in Oregon, and in a county in Florida.

The proposal in Colorado was the most far reaching because it amended the Colorado Constitution to deny forever civil rights protection to lesbians and gays. By amending the state constitution, the proposal overturned existing civil rights laws in several Colorado cities, including Denver and Boulder. Immediately after the antigay victories, civil rights supporters challenged the measures in court.

On May 20, 1996, the U.S. Supreme Court declared the Colorado measure to be unconstitutional in a case known as *Romer v. Evans*. The 6-3 vote by the Supreme Court was the most significant victory in the history of the lesbian and gay civil rights movement. The decision was considered to be particularly significant because it was written by Justice Anthony M. Kennedy, a conservative appointed to the Court by a conservative Republican president, Ronald Reagan. Joining Kennedy in the majority were justices John Paul Stevens, Sandra Day O'Connor, David Souter, Ruth Bader Ginsburg, and Stephen Breyer. Justices Antonin Scalia, Clarence Thomas, and Chief Justice William Rehnquist disagreed with the majority and issued a dissenting opinion.

"The decision was a strong statement, coming from a conservative member of a basically conservative court, that prejudice is not a valid justification for a policy that singles out gay people for special burdens not placed on others," wrote *New York Times* correspondent Linda Greenhouse.[1]

The full impact of the Supreme Court decision may not be known for years. Although the decision was a great victory for civil rights supporters, it was also limited. The decision did not tell cities or states that they have to provide civil rights protection for lesbians and gays. The decision did not overturn the Supreme Court's 1986 decision that upheld sodomy laws (see Chapter 4). The decision did not guarantee that lesbians and gays will win any of the other legal cases currently attacking antigay laws, including cases challenging the ban on homosexuals in the military and lawsuits involving same-sex marriage. As Greenhouse wrote in the *Times*, the decision provided "a constitutional shield rather than a sword."[2]

Despite the legal limitations of the decision, it did signal an important change in the attitudes of the justices. Coming exactly ten years after the Supreme Court upheld sodomy laws in the *Bowers v. Hardwick* decision, the Colorado decision spoke of lesbian and gay Americans with new respect.

"It did speak with an implicit respect for homosexuals as a group that deserves to be heard," wrote Tony Mauro in *USA Today*.[3]

Georgetown law professor Chai Feldblum, a former law clerk at the Supreme Court, said the decision signaled a change in the court. "This is a very different court from 10 years ago," she said. "This is a Court that was able to look at the law without an overlay of prejudice."[4]

THE EVIDENCE

Discrimination

Lesbians, gays, and bisexuals suffer discrimination in all aspects of their lives. The National Gay and Lesbian Task Force reports that twenty-one different polls taken over an eleven-year period found that as many as 75 percent of those surveyed concealed their sexual orientation to avoid discrimination. As many as 22 percent of the lesbians and gays surveyed reported some form of discrimination in employment. As many as 32 percent said they had faced discrimination in renting.[5] Other studies show even more problems. A poll of nine hundred lesbians and gays in Kansas City, Missouri, by the Mayor's Commission on Lesbian and Gay Concerns found that nearly 40 percent of open homosexuals reported job discrimination.[6]

Even heterosexuals can be hurt by antigay bias. Vernon Jantz is a heterosexual who was a substitute teacher in Wichita, Kansas. Despite the fact that he is married, Jantz was denied a full-time job because the school principal thought he had "homosexual tendencies." Many other examples of discrimination exist.

Joyce Perciballi of Canton, Ohio, was fired from her job as a manager at a Fortune 500 company after her supervisor learned she was a lesbian. Before her sexual orientation became known, Perciballi had been promoted frequently, advancing from a job as clerk to a manager's position.

A University of Alabama graduate student, John Howard, was a tour guide at a regional paper company. One day his supervisor called Howard into his office and said Howard's work was "perfect." The supervisor then asked Howard about his sexual orientation. When Howard said he is gay and the president of a gay group at the university, he was fired.[7]

One of the most famous cases of discrimination occurred at the Cracker Barrel Country Store and Restaurant chain, which operates 163 facilities in the Southeast. In 1991, Cracker Barrel vice president William A. Bridges issued a memo ordering each restaurant to fire its lesbian and gay workers because they did not live up to "traditional American values."[8] When Cracker Barrel cook Cheryl Summerville was fired from a restaurant near Atlanta, she received a notice that read:

> This employee is being terminated due to violation of
> company policy. This employee is Gay.[9]

Summerville said about a dozen workers were fired at her restaurant for being gay. After publicity about the firings, executives at Cracker Barrel said they were reconsidering the anti-gay policy. Before this could happen, however, company shareholders defeated a proposal to ban discrimination based on sexual orientation.[10]

The Constitution and Lesbian and Gay Americans

Until the Supreme Court's 1996 decision in the Colorado case, the U.S. Constitution was "little more than a promise" to lesbian and gay citizens and heterosexuals who are mistakenly thought to be gay.[11] Courts have ruled repeatedly that neither the U.S. Constitution nor existing civil rights laws protect any American from discrimination based on sexual orientation. Despite the victory lesbian and gay citizens won in the Supreme Court's 1996 decision, the decision is so limited that Americans who suffer discrimination based on sexual orientation may still find little help from the courts. This means that unless Americans live in one of the states, cities, or counties that have passed antidiscrimination laws, both homosexuals and heterosexuals will still be helpless to fight discrimination based on sexual orientation.

For example, the heterosexual teacher in Wichita, Vernon Jantz, filed a lawsuit after he was refused employment for supposedly "looking" like he was gay. Even though he was heterosexual, Jantz lost his case because the court ruled that there is no protection against employment discrimination based on sexual orientation.

In Detroit, a federal court ruled that a gay postal worker who had been harassed at work and beaten was not protected under the 1964 Civil Rights Act. The judge wrote that "homosexuality is not an impermissible [illegal] criteria on which to discriminate. . . . These actions, although cruel, are not made illegal."[12] In an Arizona employment discrimination case, a judge instructed a jury that "an employee is not wrongfully terminated if he is fired solely for being homosexual."[13]

The Issue of "Special Rights"
The central argument used to attack civil rights laws involves a concept opponents call "special rights." Opponents argue that lesbians and gays want to pass laws that will make homosexuals more powerful than heterosexuals. "Special rights" has been an effective campaign slogan. To many legal scholars, however—including a majority of the U.S. Supreme Court—the concept of "special rights" is simply false.

The argument over "special rights" was at the heart of the Supreme Court's 1996 decision in *Romer v. Evans*. Matt Coles, director of the Lesbian and Gay Rights Project of the American Civil Liberties Union, said the Supreme Court appeared to "go out of its way to take on the 'special rights' rhetoric."[14] Writing for the majority, Justice Kennedy rejected the opponent's argument that Colorado's Amendment 2 had taken only "special rights" away from homosexual citizens. "We cannot accept the view that Amendment 2's prohibition on specific legal protections does no more than deprive homosexuals of special rights," Kennedy wrote. "To the contrary, the amendment imposes a special disability upon those persons alone."[15]

Kennedy wrote that homosexual citizens would have a "special disability" because they would be the only citizens of Colorado who would have to win approval of a constitutional amendment to get civil rights protections. "We find nothing special in the protections Amendment 2 withholds," Justice Kennedy wrote. "These are protections taken for granted by most people either because they already have them or do not need them; these are protections against exclusion from an almost limitless number of transactions and endeavors that constitute ordinary civil life in a free society."[16]

Kennedy concluded, "Amendment 2 classifies homosexuals not to further a proper legislative end but to make them unequal to everyone else. This Colorado cannot do. A state cannot so deem a class of persons a stranger to its laws. Amendment 2 violates the Equal Protection Clause."[17]

Even though the Supreme Court declared "special rights" to be an absurd concept, opponents continue to use it to attack lesbian and gay Americans. In fact, "special rights" remains an effective campaign slogan. Why? The answer lies in the power of stereotypes. The stereotype of a homosexual paints a picture of a fiendish, driven predator who either molests children or preys on naive adults. If the stereotype were true and every lesbian, gay, and bisexual American acted like that, then every one of them would be guilty of the worst kind of crime, a felony. Under U.S. law, people who are guilty of felonies do not have equal rights with the rest of Americans. At the very least, felons are imprisoned and lose the right to vote. If the stereotype were true, then homosexual Americans would be asking for something special when they ask to be treated equally with heterosexuals.

The problem with the stereotype is that it isn't true. Even though prejudice and lack of information allows some people to continue to believe in the stereotype, the reality is that being gay does not make someone act in a certain way. Being a homosexual does not make a person a child molester any more than being a heterosexual turns a person into a molester. (See Chapter 4 for a discussion of scientific studies that have identified heterosexual males as the largest known group of child molesters.) Some lesbians and gays do commit crimes, but that does not mean that all homosexuals commit crimes. Declaring that all homosexuals are criminals condemns the law-abiding citizens along with the felons. This is just as bad as declaring all heterosexuals are felons because some are kidnappers, rapists, and murderers. Finally, a long-standing principle of American law declares that people can be punished for their conduct, but not for their status. This is the deepest meaning of the constitutional right of "equal protection under the law." In other words, any American who kills, rapes, kidnaps, or steals—whether that individual is heterosexual or homosexual—is a criminal. People's actions, not their sexual orientations, make them criminals.

Perhaps the most confusing aspect of this debate is the fact that opponents cite so-called scientific data that makes the stereotypes about homosexuals appear to be true. The material is misleading because it appears to come from credible scientists. The studies are not based on science, however. They are not produced by credible scientists. Many of these studies have been published by the Family Research Institute and its founder, Paul Cameron, who was trained as a psychologist. Scientists have repeatedly condemned Cameron's methods and his ethics. Cameron has been punished for unethical conduct and the misuse of data by the American Psychological Association, the American Sociological Association, and the Nebraska Psychological Association.[18]

Civil Rights Laws and Affirmative Action

Sometimes opponents argue that civil rights laws would force churches to hire lesbian, gay, or bisexual ministers through affirmative action programs. However, legal experts say this argument is as much a lie as the concept of "special rights." In fact, most civil rights laws specifically exempt churches and other religious organizations from having to do what the laws say.

Furthermore, lesbians and gays have never been included in affirmative action programs, which are designed to help African-Americans and other minorities get ahead economically. Affirmative action has never been a component of the lesbian and gay civil rights movement. To guard against misunderstandings, most laws protecting the civil rights of lesbians and gays passed today include language that specifically exempts lesbians and gays from being included in affirmative action.

The Impact of *Bowers v. Hardwick*

Often civil rights opponents argue that the U.S. Supreme Court's *Bowers v. Hardwick* decision makes it impossible to pass laws banning discrimination based on sexual orientation. The *Bowers v. Hardwick* decision upheld the constitutionality of sodomy laws—laws that make homosexual sex between consenting adults a criminal offense (see Chapter 4).

Legal experts, however, say that *Bowers v. Hardwick* is a limited decision that covers only sodomy laws. Nothing in the decision touched on the issue of protection from discrimination. Since the Supreme Court issued the *Bowers v. Hardwick* decision in 1986, courts have ruled repeatedly that laws protecting homosexuals from discrimination are constitutional even in states that have sodomy laws. Rhode Island is one example of a state that has both a sodomy law and a law banning discrimination based on sexual orientation.

The Law, Religion, and Parental Rights

Another opposition argument concerns parental rights and freedom of religion. Opponents argue that if antidiscrimination laws are passed, then parents and churches will no longer be able to teach their own values.

Legal experts disagree, however. Legal scholars report that civil rights laws deal with only one issue—the public, commercial activity of individuals, and the government. Private activities, including the activities of a parent or a church, are not affected. Furthermore, most civil rights laws now include exemptions for religious groups.

"How do we insure constitutional equality and at the same time recognize individual freedom?" asked Suzanne Goldberg, an attorney with the Lambda Legal Defense and Education Fund. "I think that the answer is basically that while people are free to pick and choose their friends, the question is a different one when we are talking about commercial interactions or transactions. There, it is for the government to insure equal opportunity for all people."[19]

Many legal scholars believe that the only people who are trying to limit the religious freedom and the parental rights of Americans are civil rights opponents. For example, the anti-gay proposals passed in Cincinnati, Colorado, Florida, and Oregon attempt to impose the beliefs of opponents on every American.

The Colorado Supreme Court noted, "While it is true that parents have a constitutionally protected interest in inculcating [implanting] their children with their own values . . . defendants point to no authority, and we are aware of none, holding that parents have the corresponding right of insuring that government endorses those values."[20]

The Impact of Antigay Proposals on All Minorities

Many legal experts believe that antigay proposals are dangerous for all minorities. These proposals are so frightening that many civil rights organizations joined the fight against them. When the Colorado proposal went before the U.S. Supreme Court, many civil rights groups joined lesbians and gays to ask the Supreme Court to overturn it. Among those groups are the National Association for the Advancement of Colored People Legal Defense and Education Fund, which was one of the leaders of the fight to win equal rights for African-Americans. Other civil rights groups included the Asian American Legal Defense and Education Fund, the Puerto Rican Legal Defense and Education Fund, the National Council of la Raza, the Japanese American Citizens League, the Mexican American Legal Defense Fund, and the Women's Legal Defense Fund.[21]

Among the strongest opponents of antigay proposals is the National Bar Association, a 20,000-member organization of lawyers dedicated to promoting justice for African-Americans and other economically disadvantaged people. In a brief submitted to the Supreme Court, the National Bar Association argued that the arguments used to defend the Colorado proposal were similar to the arguments racists used to support racist laws. More than that, the Colorado proposal opens up all minorities for discrimination because it gives racists a way to discriminate legally.

"[Colorado's] Amendment 2 would allow individuals to discriminate against citizens merely because an individual thinks the other is gay," the National Bar Association wrote in its brief. "Thus, under Amendment 2, a bigoted employer could deny a position to any African-American by simply asserting that he thought the applicant was homosexual, while the actual reason may be race based. Enforcement of any antidiscrimination laws would become almost impossible."[22]

Civil Rights and Popular Polls

One way to win a political campaign is to convince the opposing side that victory is impossible. Civil rights opponents often say that lesbians and gays have little support, but the evidence tells a different story. A survey by *Newsweek* magazine is only one of many polls showing that Americans overwhelmingly support legal protection for lesbians and gays. Nearly 80 percent of the people polled by *Newsweek* said homosexuals should have equal rights in job opportunities. Only 17 percent said they should not.[23]

With such strong support for lesbians and gays, it seems strange that civil rights opponents have won so many victories. However, their success may stem from the fact that Americans are confused. For example, one poll showed that 74 percent of Americans favor preventing job discrimination against gays at the same time that 80 percent believe that lesbian and gay Americans are covered by current civil rights laws.[24]

As the debate over antidiscrimination laws has continued, government officials on both the state and federal level have shown their support for civil rights for lesbians and gays. The Internal Revenue Service included protection against discrimination based on sexual orientation in its contract with its more than 90,000 employees in 1989.[25] In 1992, Louisiana governor Edwin Edwards signed an executive order banning antigay bias in state agencies, making Louisiana the first state in the Southeast to have such a policy. That same year, a judge in Texas declared the Dallas Police Department's ban on hiring lesbians and gays to be unconstitutional under the Texas constitution.[26]

Businesses ranging from the largest to the smallest have also adopted policies banning discrimination based on sexual orientation. The National Lesbian and Gay Task Force reports that more than 150 major corporations ban this kind of discrimination, including AT&T; Aetna Life and Casualty Co.; Apple Computer; Bank of America; CBS, Inc.; Dun & Bradstreet Corp.; Eastman Kodak Co.; General Motors Corp.; IBM; Levi Strauss Associates, Inc.; Marriott, Inc.; Microsoft; New York Life; and Sears & Roebuck.[27]

Supporters of a recent federal antidiscrimination bill read like a listing in *Who's Who in America*. Those supporters include President Bill Clinton, retired senator Barry Goldwater (R–Arizona), the AFL-CIO, the United Steel Workers of America, the Service Employees International Union, the National Council of Churches, the Episcopal Church, and the Evangelical Lutheran Church in America. The bill has been championed by the Leadership Conference on Civil Rights, the nation's largest civil rights coalition, representing more than 185 organizations.

Even many members of Congress have begun to support lesbians and gays. A majority of House members and nearly two-thirds of the Senate signed a pledge in 1994 declaring that they will not engage in discrimination based on sexual orientation in hiring, promoting, or firing congressional employees.[28]

The Impact of Civil Rights Laws

Probably the best places to look for evidence on the impact of antidiscrimination laws are cities where the laws have passed. Joyce Purnick, a writer for *The New York Times*, focused on one major city in 1996 when she examined the impact of an antidiscrimination law passed by the New York City Council in 1986.[29] Purnick found that the law had caused so few problems that ten of the fourteen council members who originally voted against it said they would now be inclined to vote for it. One member said he would still vote against it. Three of the council members who voted no could not be reached.

"The city hasn't folded, the sky didn't fall down. I don't see where it hurts at all," Councilman Jerome O'Donovan of Staten Island said.

Many people told Purnick about how much the law has helped. While they were aware that an antidiscrimination law cannot end prejudice, it can give people a sense that they have rights.

"What we see in [gay] youth is so different," said Frances Kunreuther, executive director of the Hetrick-Martin Institute, an organization for lesbian, gay, and bisexual youth. "We had to protect young frightened teenagers. Today they are not cowering in the corner anymore."[30]

CHAPTER 6

BATTLEGROUND: THE MILITARY

THE ISSUE

Should gays and lesbians be allowed to serve openly in the military?

THE ARGUMENTS

The ban on homosexuals in the military must be maintained.

> **1.** Homosexuals cannot control themselves sexually. In the military, everyone lives and works together. Open homosexuals would prey on others, particularly on young, naive recruits.
> **2.** Even if homosexuals are not sexual predators, their presence will disrupt the morale and comradeship of fighting units. Homosexuals are so hated that other soldiers and sailors will never accept them.
> **3.** The presence of homosexuals will spread AIDS in the military.
> **4.** Homosexuals are mentally ill. They are too weak emotionally and physically to perform in the military.
> **5.** Homosexuals are a security risk because they can be blackmailed.

The ban must be lifted.

> **1.** The military should judge citizens on their individual abilities and actions and not on their sexual orientation.

97

2. Lesbians and gays have served with honor and distinction in the U.S. military since the Revolutionary War. They are asking only to be allowed to serve openly and to be freed from the military's antigay witch-hunts.

3. Other nations allow gays to serve in the military. Their militaries do not suffer.

4. Lesbians and gays who serve openly cannot be blackmailed because they have nothing to hide.

5. The ban on gays is based on stereotypes and prejudice.

6. The ban makes it easier to sexually harass women in the military.

7. The investigations and separation of thousands of highly trained and capable soldiers, sailors, airmen, and marines have cost American taxpayers millions of dollars and drained the military of needed personnel.

8. The military doesn't even believe its own arguments. In times of war, commanders allow lesbians and gays to serve openly.

THE SITUATION

In late 1992, the military's ban on homosexuals became the first gay issue to be the center of a national debate. The issue erupted when the newly elected president, Bill Clinton, said he would keep his campaign promise to end the ban. The controversy headlined the news for months. Congress held hearings. The Joint Chiefs of Staff, the leaders of the U.S. military, announced their opposition to lifting the ban. A Navy pilot announced that he is gay on the ABC-TV show "Nightline." Immediately afterward, the Navy moved to discharge the pilot. A Marine officer told a congressional hearing that he favored the ban, while his gay son testified that he wanted the ban lifted. Congressmen toured a submarine and posed for photos with sailors who said they were afraid to serve with gays. Other heterosexual servicemen told a congressional committee that they had served with gays in the past and would be proud to serve with them in the future.

The controversy was finally resolved when Clinton and Congress agreed on a new policy known as "Don't Ask, Don't Tell." Under the old ban, investigators actively searched for gays and lesbians in the military. Military personnel could be discharged for any evidence of homosexuality or suspected homosexual tendencies. Being friends with a gay man or lesbian or reading a book with gay characters was enough to get someone kicked out of the military. Under "Don't Ask, Don't Tell," the military is not supposed to ask about an individual's sexual orientation, while lesbians and gays are not supposed to talk about their private lives.

The debate over "Don't Ask, Don't Tell" is not the first time the ban has been challenged. The names of the people who fought the ban are too numerous to list. They include Air Force sergeant Leonard Matlovich, who wrote to his commanding officer in 1975 saying that he was gay. Miriam Ben-Shalom, a member of the U.S. Army Reserve, fought her discharge in court for nearly fifteen years. She did not give up until the U.S. Supreme Court refused to hear her case. By the 1980s and 1990s, the ban on gays in the military had become an issue on college campuses. At that time, students at fifty universities campaigned unsuccessfully to kick the Reserve Officer Training Corps (ROTC) off-campus. ROTC recruits college students to become officers and trains them on-campus.

No one knows the exact number of people who have been discharged or forced to resign because of accusations of homosexuality. *Time* magazine reported that as many as 100,000 members of the military may have been forced out since World War II. The military reported that in one decade (the 1980s) 16,919 service members were discharged for homosexuality.[1] These figures are misleading, however, because they do not include the number of officers who were allowed to resign. No accurate figures exist reflecting that number, but military insiders report that every antigay investigation has an enormous impact. For example, the official result of a 1988 investigation of lesbians at the Parris Island Marine Corps Recruitment Depot in South Carolina was the discharge of eighteen women. Three women were sent to prison. Unofficially, insiders at Parris Island said the investigation led to the loss of about sixty-five marines, including women who decided not to reenlist and officers who resigned.[2]

Massive antigay investigations have been carried out at practically every military base and among every unit in the U.S. Army, Navy, Air Force, Marines, and Coast Guard. Among those targeted have been a Strategic Air Command base in Michigan, the U.S. Military Academy at West Point, and the Army's elite Old Guard unit, which guards the Tomb of the Unknown Soldier and performs ceremonies at the White House.

Suspected lesbians and gays have been followed by investigators and awakened in the middle of the night as investigators burst into their quarters to try to catch them in the act. Investigators have routinely held suspects for days, and even locked them in closets for hours. Investigators have threatened lesbians with the loss of custody of their children and threatened to harass suspects' parents. Always the investigators' goal has been to force the suspect not only to confess but to name other gays and lesbians. Once a suspect provides a list, each person on the list is subjected to the same treatment until each confesses and provides another list of names.[3]

The exact cost of the military's ban on homosexuality is impossible to determine, but even the government admits that the price is high. The General Accounting Office of the U.S. Congress reported that the military spends $27 million in just one year to enforce the ban on gays. The cost includes the money spent to investigate and process discharges and the loss of highly skilled personnel who had to be replaced. Other estimates put the cost at hundreds of millions of dollars a year.[4]

The investigations also have a human cost. Successful careers have been cut short. Friendships have been ruined. Heterosexual soldiers have been demoted for testifying in support of gay friends in discharge hearings. People have committed suicide. Others have been imprisoned for doing nothing more than having sex with a consenting adult in private. Many examples exist. Air Force lieutenant Joann Newak spent fifteen months in the military prison at Fort Leavenworth, Kansas, in the early 1980s. In 1986, an appeals court vindicated her by declaring that the military had violated her civil rights. By the time the appeals court threw out her conviction, however, Newak had already served her time in prison. Another imprisoned gay was Air Force captain Paul Star, who served nine months in Fort Leavenworth in the late 1980s.[5]

The future of the new "Don't Ask, Don't Tell" policy is uncertain. A federal district judge has ruled that the new policy is unconstitutional. Judge Eugene H. Nickerson of Brooklyn said the policy is based on fear and prejudice and violates the free speech rights of lesbians and gays. The government immediately appealed the decision. The case is continuing to go through the courts.

The History of Lesbians and Gays in the Military

Homosexuals have been daring military leaders and effective warriors throughout history. Historians report that among the many homosexual military leaders were Richard the Lion-Hearted (1157–1199) and King Frederick II of Prussia (1712–1786). Alexander the Great (356–323 B.C.) led armies that conquered Greece, the Persian Empire, and Egypt.

In the U.S. military, gay men and lesbians have a long history of service.[6] Some historians believe that America might never have won the Revolutionary War if not for the help of one Prussian-born gay general, Baron Friedrich Wilhelm Ludolf Gerhard Augustin von Steuben (1730–1794). Steuben arrived in America in early 1778 to find a demoralized Continental Army camped at Valley Forge. His task was to bring training and discipline to the disorganized army. Steuben wrote a training manual and personally drilled soldiers. George Washington later appointed Steuben the first inspector general of the Army, and Congress commissioned him as a major general. Steuben also commanded a division at Yorktown.

Other gay heroes of the American military include Navy officers Stephen Decatur and Richard Somers, who were lovers. Somers was killed in 1804 fighting the Barbary pirates off Tripoli in what is now Libya. Decatur became a hero in the War of 1812 and retired with the rank of commodore.

In the modern military, gay men and lesbians have served honorably for decades.[7] Homosexuals served and died in World War I, World War II, Korea, and Vietnam. The efforts of homosexuals in Vietnam, however, is probably the best documented.

Army lieutenant Jerry Rosanbalm served as an intelli-

gence officer in Vietnam and was wounded during the Tet
Offensive in 1968. His lover, Don Winn, died in the war to
become one of the many gay men whose names would later
appear on the Vietnam Memorial. Air Force captain Jim
Dressel flew F-14 fighters in Vietnam and was awarded the
Distinguished Flying Cross and a dozen other medals.
Leonard Matlovich, who was later to challenge the military's
antigay policy in court, was decorated with a Commendation
Medal and the Bronze Star in 1966 during his first tour of
duty in Vietnam. On his second tour in Vietnam, Matlovich
was wounded. During her time in Vietnam, Margarethe Cammermeyer was awarded a Bronze Star, a Meritorious Service
Medal, and two Army Achievement medals. Colonel Cammermeyer would later fight her discharge for being a lesbian.

Today, lesbians and gays continue play a key role in the
U.S. military. In a five-year investigation that included interviews with 1,100 people and accumulated 15,000 pages of
documents, journalist Randy Shilts found that gays and lesbians have graduated from every one of the military acade-
mies and at least one gay man has served in the astronaut
program. Gays have served as generals or admirals in every
branch of the armed forces. At least one gay man has served
on the Joint Chiefs of Staff. Gays have jumped with the
101st Airborne paratroopers. At least one gay admiral has
commanded a fleet.

At the same time that the U.S. military spent millions of
dollars to discharge lesbians and gays, other countries have
had no problems allowing lesbians and gays to serve openly.
Among the countries that allow homosexuals to serve are the
Netherlands, Denmark, Australia, France, and Israel. Israel
once limited the involvement of lesbians and gays to certain
jobs. Since 1993, however, Israel has opened all positions,
including combat, to lesbians and gays.

Pentagon Studies and Pentagon Reasoning

The Pentagon's own studies do not support the ban on gays in the military. Three findings are obvious from a series of studies completed over a period of forty years:

1. Lesbians and gays are as qualified—or more qualified—than heterosexuals.

2. Lesbians and gays do not create problems in their units.

3. Lesbians and gays are not a security risk.

A 1957 study determined that homosexuality did not affect either people's abilities or their level of success in the military. The study noted that there was no "supporting data" to the idea that "homosexual individuals and those who have indulged in homosexual behavior cannot acceptably serve in the military." There was also no evidence that gays were more likely than heterosexuals to reveal secrets.[8] A 1989 study by the Defense Personnel Security Research and Education Center declared that allowing lesbians and gays to serve openly would not disrupt military discipline or morale. The concerns of generals were based on fear—and not reality, the study noted.

Even when the military is working to discharge lesbians and gays, commanders still recognize their competence and skill. A 1990 U.S. Navy memo ordering an investigation of lesbians on board ships noted that it would be difficult to identify lesbians because they were "among the command's top professionals."[9]

Despite the evidence of their own studies, Pentagon leaders have continued their antigay policies. Decades ago, the Pentagon said lesbians and gays had to be discharged because they were criminals. Later the Pentagon called lesbians and gays security risks. At other times, lesbians and gays have been declared to be mentally or physically unfit. One by one, military leaders have abandoned these reasons. Today only one reason remains. Now, Pentagon generals and admirals declare that the antigay policy is necessary because allowing lesbians and gays to serve openly would lower morale and lead soldiers to fight among themselves. All of this would lower a unit's readiness for combat. The Pentagon's antigay policy is based on the Pentagon's fear of the actions of heterosexuals—not on its fear of the actions of homosexuals. These reasons are nearly identical to the arguments racists made in the 1940s when they fought the integration of African-American soldiers into all-white military units.[10] The 1989 report attacked this reasoning as being shortsighted and based on prejudice.

Perhaps one of the best pieces of evidence for ending the ban came in the mid-1990s when at least sixteen open, acknowledged lesbians and gays served legally in the armed forces. The sixteen retained their place in the armed forces because they had filed lawsuits against the government. Judges ordered that they be allowed to serve until all of the court proceedings were completed. Some of the sixteen have served openly—and effectively—for more than two years.

"The entire theory from the government attorneys and Pentagon is that the mere presence of homosexuals will so affect the performance of heterosexuals that we need to exclude them," said C. Dixon Osburn, a lawyer with the Servicemembers Legal Defense Network, which is defending the sixteen. "This shows that is false and not based on anything factual. When there is good leadership, sexual orientation is not an issue and members are judged by performance and ability, and not by sexual orientation."[11]

The Danger of AIDS

If every lesbian and gay man serving in the U.S. armed forces magically turned purple tomorrow, then Pentagon officials could discharge every single one of them. Yet public health officials report that such an action would not control AIDS in the military. AIDS is spread by what people do—not by who people are. Throwing one group of people out of the military will not stop the disease, because the behaviors that spread AIDS are performed by both heterosexuals and homosexuals. Both heterosexuals and homosexuals carry the virus.

Health officials agree that the only way to control AIDS is for everyone—heterosexual and homosexual—to practice safer sex and avoid any behavior that might result in contacting blood or other fluids from another person's body. Oddly enough, if concern about AIDS was the real reason for the Pentagon's actions, then military commanders would be smart to recruit more lesbians. Lesbians have the smallest incidence of AIDS of any population, including heterosexuals. (For more information on AIDS, see Chapter 7.)

Sexual Harassment and the Antigay Policy

The antigay policy has caused extra problems for women—both heterosexual and homosexual. These problems have occurred as the military has gone through a revolutionary change that transformed women from being auxiliary members of the military to being on the front lines. The change began in the 1970s when the all-female branches of the U.S. military were disbanded and women were integrated into the Army, Air Force, Navy, and Marines.[12] By the end of the 1990s, women were serving in almost every military job. They were working on ships at sea and flying jets as combat pilots.

As the official policy changed, many men continued to oppose women's presence in the military. Their actions, however, were limited. They could not legally discriminate against a woman.

The situation is very different if the woman is a lesbian or a heterosexual who has been accused of being a lesbian. Often, hunts for lesbians have involved interrogation of every single woman on a base—whether or not there is evidence that a woman is a lesbian. At times, lesbians have been investigated when gay men have been ignored. For example, one gay man reported that only women were investigated during the time he served on the USS *Land*. This was despite the fact that the crew included a large and fairly open group of gay men. One of the ship's highest officers was a gay man who hosted huge parties for the ship's gay male crew. In all of the services, women are far more likely to be discharged for homosexuality than men. In 1979, women were six times more likely to be discharged from the U.S. Army for homosexuality than men.[13]

Women face another problem. If a woman turns down a man's sexual advance, then the man can accuse her of being a lesbian or force her to have sex with him by threatening to accuse her of lesbianism. If a woman complains about sexual harassment, then the man can protect himself by claiming that she is a lesbian. This strategy has been used by many men who have sexually harassed, even raped, women. Often women who complain of harassment find themselves under investigation for lesbianism, while their attackers are let alone. Meanwhile, sexual harassment remains a major problem in the military. One study found that 70 percent of women in the armed forces said they had experienced sexual harassment.[14]

Military Readiness

By kicking thousands of highly trained lesbians and gays out of the military, commanders have deprived themselves of some of their most important personnel. The 1991 Gulf War provides numerous examples. When the United States and its allies declared war on Iraq, many commanders feared that Iraq would use chemical and biological weapons. Army Reserve captain Dusty Pruitt had thirteen years of experience in teaching soldiers how to defend themselves against those weapons, yet Pruitt did not serve in the Gulf. Instead, she was in the United States battling in court to overturn her discharge for being a lesbian. The Gulf War also created a need for skilled Arab-speaking translators, but the military had a desperate shortage of Arab speakers. The shortage was at least partially the result of an antigay investigation that had forced several Arab translators out of the military. By the time the Gulf War started, the need for translators was so great that the National Security Agency contacted some of the discharged gays and asked them to help.[15]

Gays in Combat

In public debates on the ban on gays, the military has long argued that homosexuals hurt the ability of units to function in combat. In times of war, however, the military has not hesitated to send open, acknowledged homosexuals into combat. In fact, the only time that the antigay policy has not been vigorously enforced is during war.

The most recent example of this occurred during the Gulf War. On September 1, 1990, the secretary of the army ordered the service to suspend all discharges of soldiers who had "skills in short supply in the Army," including lesbians and gays. By November, orders had been issued to suspend all discharges from all the armed forces, including discharges of lesbians and gays. Commanders told lesbians and gays they were too valuable to their units to be discharged in time of war. At the same time, several lesbians and gays reported that their commanders gave them another chilling message: They could serve, fight, and even die, but if they survived, they would be discharged as soon as they returned home.[16]

THE ARMY'S FIRST OFFICIAL GAY SOLDIER

Meet Perry Watkins of Tacoma, Washington.[17] Watkins spent his entire career doing something the Pentagon says cannot be done. Watkins was a successful soldier and an openly gay man.

Drafted at the height of the Vietnam War in 1967, Watkins, an African-American, never hid his sexual orientation. When he filled out forms for his draft physical, Watkins checked "yes" when the question asked if he had "homosexual tendencies." When an Army psychiatrist asked if he was trying to get out of the Army, Watkins said he had no objections to going in and wouldn't even object to going to Vietnam. The psychiatrist declared Watkins qualified to serve. In May 1968, the U.S. Army inducted Watkins—an openly gay man.

For the rest of his career, Watkins was repeatedly promoted and praised. He served throughout the world, including in Europe and Korea, where he performed in combat conditions and did duty in a foxhole. By 1980, he had been promoted to staff sergeant and had been appointed supervisor for his battalion's personnel center at Fort Lewis near his hometown of Tacoma.

Although the Army tried repeatedly to discharge Watkins for being gay, they failed for years to force him out. Watkins always fought back, sometimes with attorneys and always by refusing to give investigators the names of other gays. Most often, Watkins had the strong support of the other men in his unit.

For example, during one discharge attempt in 1975 in Korea, First Sergeant Owen Johnson testified at a hearing that he knew Watkins was gay. Johnson said he would be happy to work with Watkins again.

"Everyone in the company knows that Watkins is a homosexual," Johnson told the hearing. "There have been no complaints or trouble."

The hearing board in Korea ruled unanimously to keep Watkins in the Army.

"There is no evidence suggesting that his [Watkins's] behavior has had either a degrading effect upon unit performance, morale or discipline or upon its own job performance," the ruling read.[18]

In 1981, the Army used Watkins's homosexuality as a reason to revoke his security clearance. By 1984, the Army was able to finally discharge Watkins for being gay. The Army's victory, however, did not last. The Ninth Circuit Court of Appeals in San Francisco ordered the Army to reinstate Watkins. The appeals court said it was unfair to discharge Watkins after years of promoting him and allowing him to reenlist, particularly because Watkins had always been open about his homosexuality. Soon afterwards, the U.S. Supreme Court refused to hear the case, giving Watkins the final legal victory he needed. A year later, Watkins accepted a settlement from the Army. The settlement included retroactive pay of about $135,000, full retirement benefits, honorable discharge, and retroactive promotion from staff sergeant to sergeant first class.

Because the Watkins case involved such a narrow point—the issue of fairness—it did not set a precedent for other gay and lesbian soldiers. But Watkins's victory was an historic one. In effect, the highest court in the land had ordered the Army to let an openly gay man serve.

CHAPTER 7

BATTLEGROUND:
AIDS AND GAY RIGHTS

THE ISSUES

1. Are gays to blame for AIDS as civil rights opponents claim?
2. Has AIDS made homosexuals a public health threat?
3. Is AIDS God's punishment for gays?
4. Has hatred of homosexuals led the government to fail to take crucial actions that would have saved lives? Are people dying because of prejudice?

THE ARGUMENTS

AIDS is proof that homosexuals do not deserve civil rights.

1. AIDS is God's punishment of gays.
2. Gays are to blame for AIDS because their promiscuous behavior created the disease and spread it.
3. Because of AIDS, gays are a threat to public health.

The response to AIDS is proof of the prejudice faced by lesbians and gays.

1. Many religious leaders believe that viewing AIDS as punishment is absurd, unfair, and hateful—a very

"unchristian" attitude for Christians. Because AIDS also strikes heterosexuals, it can hardly be a punishment for being gay.

2. AIDS is caused by a virus that attacks heterosexuals as well as homosexuals. The origin of the virus is unknown; however, it was not created by lesbians and gays.

3. The virus that causes AIDS cannot be transmitted by casual contact. Even if it could be, most homosexuals would be no threat because most are not infected with the virus.

THE SITUATION

Nearly a quarter of a million people have died of acquired immune deficiency syndrome (AIDS) in the United States. AIDS is a disease that damages the immune system, the system that fights illness in the body. As more and more of the disease-fighting cells are destroyed, the body's defenses are weakened and infections that would not harm a healthy person can become serious illnesses. As their immune systems become increasingly weakened, people with AIDS suffer a series of illnesses, eventually ending in death. AIDS can also damage the heart and attack the nervous system, causing blindness and dementia. (Dementia is a condition often seen in people with Alzheimer's disease, where an individual loses the ability to think, understand, and remember.)

Although people have survived with AIDS for many years, no one has yet found a cure. No vaccine has been found to protect people from getting AIDS. However, some medications slow the progress of the disease. Researchers also hope that studies of long-term survivors of AIDS will help identify new ways to battle the disease.

Human immunodeficiency virus (HIV) has been identified as the cause of AIDS.[1] After getting HIV, a person may feel healthy and live an active life. NBA star Earvin "Magic" Johnson, for example, played on the gold-medal U.S. Olympic basketball team after learning that he was HIV-positive. Greg Louganis won Olympic gold medals in diving when he was HIV-positive. Some people have taken as long as fifteen years to develop symptoms of AIDS. Because AIDS can take so long to develop, many people with HIV do not even know they have the virus.

Although AIDS is deadly, it is not spread by casual contact. Tuberculosis, the common cold, and the flu are just some of the illnesses that are much easier to get than AIDS. A person infected by HIV cannot spread the disease by sneezing or coughing. A person cannot get HIV from hugging, shaking hands, swimming in pools, or using public toilets or telephones. Family members who live with people who have HIV or AIDS do not get the disease through everyday contact. Although there is no cure, the good news about AIDS is that anyone can protect himself from getting the disease by knowing how HIV is transmitted from one person to another and by taking a few precautions.

HIV is concentrated in body fluids. The highest amounts are found in blood, semen, vaginal fluids, and possibly breast milk.[2] Scientists have identified four ways in which people become infected with HIV:

1. By having unprotected sex with someone who has HIV. Unprotected sex means having sexual intercourse or oral sex without using a condom or a dental dam.[3] Health officials say that anyone—heterosexual or homosexual—who is sexually active is at risk for contracting HIV and must take precautions.

2. By sharing a needle. Drug users who inject drugs into their veins and use someone else's needle or allow someone to share their needle are at great risk. Only sterile needles are safe. Thoroughly cleaning a needle in bleach can disinfect it.

3. By using infected blood or blood products. Transfusions of blood or blood products, including clotting factors used by hemophiliacs, can spread HIV. Hemophiliacs have an illness that makes even the smallest cut a danger. Their blood does not clot and stop flowing.

4. By an infected pregnant woman's transmitting the virus to her child. HIV can be transmitted while the child is in the womb and during delivery. An infant can also be infected through breast feeding. A pregnant woman with HIV can lower the chance of transmitting the virus to her child if she takes certain medications before the child is born.

Although isolated cases of AIDS may have appeared as early as the 1950s and perhaps even earlier, the disease was not identified until the early 1980s. The first cases were identified in gay men in the United States. However, researchers later discovered that HIV had been infecting people and AIDS had been killing them in central Africa, Europe, and the Caribbean in the 1970s. Most of the cases outside of the United States are among heterosexuals.

Perhaps because it was first identified in gay men, AIDS became linked in the American news media and the public mind to homosexuals. At first, even physicians thought of it as a gay disease and dubbed it gay-related immune deficiency syndrome (GRID). Most of the American public simply thought of it as the gay plague.

In the early days of the AIDS epidemic, the disease was largely ignored by the government, the news media, and the American public. AIDS researchers had to beg for money and equipment despite the fact that they were trying to stop an epidemic. People with AIDS suddenly found they were too ill to work and even to care for themselves. At the same time, American society offered no help. Many people thought AIDS was something that happened to someone else.

In the midst of this neglect, the gay community organized to help itself. Gay Men's Health Crisis in New York City, the Shanti Project in San Francisco, the AIDS Action Committee of Boston, and AIDS Project/L.A. were just a few of the groups created by gay men and lesbians. These groups launched the first AIDS prevention campaigns, provided support for people with HIV and AIDS, and helped care for people in the final days of their illnesses. Despite the fact that these groups were organized by lesbians and gays, they also helped heterosexuals.

In 1985, the attitude of the news media and the public began to change. That year all Americans learned that they knew someone with AIDS when movie actor Rock Hudson died of the disease. First popular in the 1950s, Hudson projected the image of the rugged, heterosexual hero in his movies with Elizabeth Taylor, Doris Day, and many other stars. After his death, Americans learned that Hudson had been gay. His death made AIDS headline news and helped begin to educate the American public.

As public attitudes about AIDS began to change, leaders of the far right began to use AIDS in their attacks against lesbians and gays. TV evangelist Jerry Falwell, for example, called AIDS "the judgement of God."

"The poor homosexuals," said politician and commentator Pat Buchanan. "They have declared war on nature and now nature is exacting an awful retribution."[4] A publication of the

Moral Majority declared that AIDS meant that Americans could no longer tolerate gays and lesbians:

> *Now it turns out that homosexuals and their practices can threaten our lives, our families, our children, can influence whether or not we have elective surgery, eat in certain restaurants, visit a given city or take up a certain profession or career—all because a tiny minority flaunts its lifestyle and demands that an entire nation tolerate its diseases and grant it status as a privileged minority.*[5]

AIDS is now frequently mentioned in the ongoing debate over civil rights. In the campaigns to pass antigay proposals in Colorado, Oregon, and other states, civil rights opponents portrayed gays as carriers of disease and death. A vote for civil rights was portrayed as being the same as voting to spread AIDS.

Ironically, in 1990, gays with HIV and AIDS became the only homosexuals to win federal civil rights protection. That year Congress passed, and President George Bush signed, the Americans with Disabilities Act. The act makes it illegal to discriminate against anyone with a disability, including HIV or AIDS.

THE EVIDENCE

The Origin of AIDS

No one knows where or how AIDS originated.[6] Some researchers argue that HIV and AIDS have been present among humans for centuries and that something occurred in the 1970s to turn it into an epidemic. Other researchers believe the virus began recently in African monkeys and was transmitted to humans through scratches or bites. Some researchers believe that the origin of the virus may never be found. Scientists do agree, however, that homosexual sex did not create HIV or AIDS.

The Spread of AIDS

Civil rights opponents often claim that gays spread AIDS to the United States. The evidence, however, does not support this claim. As yet, no one can explain why gay men were the first Americans to be seen with AIDS. Some researchers now believe, however, that gays may not have been the first Americans to get it. Drug users may have contracted AIDS first through the use of dirty needles. Because addicts rarely see doctors, AIDS was not identified as an illness until gay men became ill and began to visit their physicians.[7]

So far the evidence suggests that AIDS appeared simultaneously in the 1970s in the United States, Europe, and central Africa. Researchers believe that several factors helped spread the disease.[8]

1. Governments in the United States and other countries cut funding for programs designed to identify and stop infectious diseases quickly. Reduced funding made it harder to identify AIDS. Because AIDS was not identified as a threat, people did not know they were infected and spread the disease without knowing what they were doing.

2. The blood-products business had become a worldwide industry, making it easier for a blood-borne virus to be spread between countries. Once HIV got into the supply of blood and blood products, it quickly spread through transfusions and the use of blood-clotting products by hemophiliacs. The inaction of the blood-products industry allegedly helped this happen. Soon after AIDS was identified, officials at the Centers for Disease Control met with representatives of the blood-products industry and asked that they take precautions to protect the blood supply. Industry representatives refused, however, saying there was not enough proof that AIDS was transmitted through blood. Meanwhile, people continued to be infected with HIV through the use of contaminated blood.[9]

3. Heroin use soared in the world as drug addicts shared contaminated needles. Because they were often poor and had no contact with doctors, drug addicts were among the last to learn how to prevent AIDS. Health officials were also kept from distributing clean needles or even exchanging clean needles for dirty needles by politicians who feared that voters would think needle programs encourage drug use. Meanwhile, more addicts became infected with and, in turn, passed the virus on to people who did not use drugs.

4. Needles were introduced in Africa for medical use, but a lack of funding made it impossible to maintain an adequate supply of new needles. Old needles were often reused. When people got shots to cure illnesses, they were unknowingly getting shots that would also infect them with HIV.

5. Wars helped spread HIV and AIDS. As wars broke out in central Africa, the medical system broke down. Rape and prostitution were widespread, which made it easier for AIDS to be transmitted sexually.

6. Promiscuity—the practice of having many sexual partners—increased dramatically in the 1970s among some heterosexuals and some homosexuals.

The Impact of the Prejudice

Many scientists today believe antigay prejudice also played a major role in the spread of HIV and AIDS. In effect, prejudice killed. The government saw AIDS as a "gay disease" and ignored it for several key years at the beginning of the epidemic. Lack of federal funding hampered research efforts to determine how AIDS was spread. If researchers could have solved the puzzle earlier, at least some people who became infected with HIV might never have contracted the virus. Furthermore, helping gays was seen as unimportant and politically risky by the administration of Ronald Reagan, a conservative Republican who was president at the start of the epidemic. This was because much of Reagan's support was from the religious right—the strongest opponents of civil rights for lesbians and gays.

Examples of the impact of antigay prejudice are numerous. In thirteen months in the early 1980s, the Centers for Disease Control received $1 million in funding for AIDS research. In the same amount of time, the CDC received $9 million for research on Legionnaires' disease. At this point in the epidemic, hundreds of Americans were already ill, dead, or dying of AIDS. Although it was deadly, Legionnaires' disease killed only twenty-nine people.[10]

Andrew Moss, an epidemiologist at the University of California in San Francisco, was one of the key researchers in the early days of the epidemic. He pleaded repeatedly for funding, but got no response.

"This is an actual nightmare," Moss said. "The sky is falling. We know it. You can tell them it's falling, but nobody listens."[11]

By the time research money from the U.S. government began to get to scientists in May 1983, thousands of Americans were already infected with HIV. Many more would later become infected because public health officials were not allowed to tell the public how to protect itself. Case in point, the Reagan administration did not allow its own surgeon general, C. Everett Koop, M.D., to speak in public about AIDS for five years.[12]

"No one cared because it was homosexuals who were dying," wrote Randy Shilts, a *San Francisco Chronicle* reporter who covered AIDS full-time in the 1980s. "Nobody came out and said it was all right for gays to drop dead; it was just that homosexuals didn't seem to warrant the kind of urgent concern another set of victims would engender."[13]

In 1991, a fifteen-member National AIDS Commission formed by Reagan's successor, President George Bush, issued a 165-page report that confirmed Shilts's belief. The commission criticized both the Reagan and Bush administrations for failing to take action. The report noted that the administrations were "crippled" by "disbelief, prejudice, ignorance, and fear."[14]

Heterosexuals and AIDS

HIV infection and AIDS are problems faced by everyone. By 1989, heterosexual sex was found to be the fastest-growing means of transmission of the virus. About 90 percent of new cases came from heterosexual sex.[15] Between 1992 and 1993, the number of heterosexual AIDS cases jumped by more than 110 percent in the United States.[16] In Illinois, AIDS cases involving heterosexuals rose by 41 percent in 1994, while the overall increase was only 3 percent and the increase in cases in gays and bisexuals was 9 percent.[17] In some places in the United States, such as the town of Belle Glade, Florida, heterosexuals are the primary victims of AIDS. Outside the United States, more heterosexuals than gays have HIV and AIDS. About two-thirds of the world's AIDS cases are in Africa, where the majority of victims are heterosexual.[18]

The belief that AIDS is only a gay disease is very dangerous, particularly for young heterosexuals, health officials say. Believing that they cannot get AIDS, young heterosexuals can engage in high-risk behavior and end up becoming infected with HIV.[19]

Homosexuals and AIDS

Although gay and bisexual men continue to be infected with HIV, the epidemic among the U.S. gay community may have peaked in the middle 1980s. The 26,840 AIDS cases reported in 1992 among gay and bisexual adult men was only nineteen more than the number reported the year before.[20] The percentage of HIV-infected gay and bisexual men dropped 20 percent between the late 1980s and the early 1990s as gay-run campaigns taught gay men how to protect themselves.[21]

AIDS has had a tremendous impact on the lesbian and gay community. It has both devastated the community and drawn it together. AIDS has helped energize gay men to participate in politics and work for civil rights. Volunteer groups such as Gay Men's Health Crisis and the Shanti Project have drawn together gays, lesbians, and heterosexuals. For example, more than 3,000 people provided more than 530,000 hours of volunteer work to AIDS agencies in the San Francisco area in 1990.

AIDS as God's Punishment

One more point is important. If AIDS is God's punishment (and not simply a disease caused by a virus), then it is likely that the group with the lowest incidence of AIDS must be God's most favored people. If this is true, then lesbians must truly be God's chosen. Although lesbians can get AIDS and must remember to take the same precautions everyone must take, lesbians have the lowest rate of AIDS of any population—including heterosexuals.

THE FACE OF AIDS

The face of AIDS and HIV infection can be anyone's face. Every age, race, and economic class gets HIV and AIDS. Some people with the illness are heterosexual. Some are homosexual.

Angela Diya was eleven in 1994 when she faced a video camera and told her school in northern Palm Beach, Florida, that she was HIV-positive. Angela wore her orange safety-patrol belt, looked into the camera, and described the disease. She told the camera that she was worried about losing her friends.[22] Brian Hall, thirty-eight, was the director of professional services for the Epilepsy Foundation of Greater Chicago before he died of AIDS. He was called a "remarkable individual" by coworkers and was once named "Volunteer of the Year" by an antiviolence project in the Chicago area.[23] Elizabeth Glaser was forty-seven when she died of AIDS. The wife of actor Paul Michael Glaser, she was an activist for children with AIDS. Her daughter, Ariel, died of AIDS in 1988 and her son, Jake, ten at the time of his mother's death, had already tested positive for the virus.[24] AIDS has already taken the lives of many other people:

- PATRICK LIPPERT, who headed the national youth voter registration drive called Rock the Vote in 1992;
- PEDRO ZAMORA, an AIDS activist who appeared on "The Real World" on MTV;
- EMILE ARDOLINO, an Oscar-winning movie director whose credits included *Sister Act* and *Dirty Dancing;*
- MICHAEL PETERS, who won a Tony award for choreographing *Dreamgirls*, a 1981 Broadway hit, and helped create Michael Jackson's "Thriller" video;
- DR. STEPHEN M. KRITSICK, a veterinarian who became well known for his popular pet-care segments on ABC's program "Good Morning America";
- Clothes designer PERRY ELLIS; and
- FREDDIE MERCURY, lead singer of the British rock group Queen.

CHAPTER 8

BATTLEGROUND:
LESBIAN AND GAY FAMILIES

THE ISSUES

1. Should lesbians and gays keep custody of their own children?

2. Should lesbian and gay couples be allowed to be foster parents or to adopt children?

3. Should lesbian and gay couples be allowed to marry?

THE ARGUMENTS

Homosexuals have no right to a family.

1. Lesbians and gays are inherently sick and prey on children. Giving them custody of children opens those children up to sexual abuse. They cannot raise healthy children.

2. Lesbian and gay "families" cannot provide appropriate role models for their children. The children are likely to turn out to be gay.

3. It is unfair to the children to allow lesbians and gays to be their parents because the children will be stigmatized and harassed by others.

4. Homosexuals don't feel love like heterosexuals do. Homosexuals do not form close emotional bonds in the same way that heterosexuals do. Homosexuals are wildly promiscuous.

5. It is against God's law for gays to marry.

6. Because gays cannot procreate, their relationships can never be considered to be a marriage—either legally or in the eyes of God.

Homosexuals should have family rights.

1. Homosexuality is not an illness. Like heterosexuals, homosexuals vary in their ability to parent. Some are good parents and some are bad parents. Lesbian and gay parents should be judged individually.

2. The children of lesbians and gays are no more likely to be mentally ill than the children of heterosexuals. Children of homosexuals are also not more likely to be gay.

3. Prejudice and discrimination are difficult for anyone to face. To say that prejudice disqualifies lesbians and gays as parents is also to say that African-Americans should not be parents because racism exists.

4. Lesbians and gays love and form deep and lasting commitments just like heterosexuals. To claim otherwise is to declare that lesbians and gays are somehow not human and to ignore the reality of their lives.

5. Some people say God forbids gay marriages, but not all churches agree. Some churches perform lesbian and gay marriages.

6. The ability to procreate is not a requirement for marriage in the United States. Heterosexual couples can legally marry even if they do not want children or know that they are biologically unable to have children.

125

Issues involving family and lesbians and gays are among the most emotional questions under debate. Civil rights opponents often base their opposition to all civil rights laws by arguing that homosexuals are trying to destroy the heterosexual family. Robert H. Knight of the Family Research Council has attacked same-sex couples as being nothing more than a "counterfeit version" of marriage.

"Counterfeit versions drive out the real thing," Knight said. "Gay rights enacted into law becomes tyranny for those who favor traditional sexual morality."[1]

Civil rights supporters argued that their opponents are hypocrites.

"We're labeled as promiscuous, but when we ask for recognition of our long-term relationships, we're denied," said Robert Bray of the National Gay and Lesbian Task Force.[2]

Americans are divided in their attitudes on family rights. One poll sponsored by *Newsweek* magazine found that Americans overwhelmingly support giving same-sex spouses many of the same tax and legal benefits as heterosexual spouses. Seventy percent of the people polled approved of inheritance rights for lesbian and gay spouses, 67 percent approved of health insurance, and 58 percent approved of giving Social Security benefits to lesbian and gay spouses.[3] Only 35 percent, however, approved of allowing lesbians and gays to legally marry. Only 32 percent approved of allowing same-sex spouses to adopt their spouses' children.[4]

Currently, lesbians and gay men have no legal protections for their families. Same-sex couples are not allowed to marry in any of the fifty states. The impact of this touches every aspect of the lives of lesbians and gays. This means that a lesbian or gay man whose partner is injured or ill has no right to visit that person in the hospital or participate in medical decisions. If the partner dies, the surviving partner has no right to plan or even to attend the funeral and no automatic right to inherit property. In most companies, the surviving partner does not even have the right to take a day off from work to attend the funeral, let alone to take time off to grieve. In most companies, lesbian and gay partners cannot get health insurance or other benefits that are commonly given to heterosexual spouses.

Many lesbians and gay men are also parents, yet they have little or no protection for their children. Children have been taken away from lesbians and gay men for no other reason than the fact that they were homosexual. Sometimes lesbian mothers and gay fathers have been forbidden to visit their children or to have their children spend the night in their house. All of this has happened despite a lesbian or gay man's ability to be a parent and despite her or his past record as a parent.

The most famous case involves Sharon Bottoms, who lost custody of her young son, Tyler, in Virginia. Bottoms's mother filed for custody of her grandson after Bottoms exchanged vows with her life partner, April Wade.[5] In ruling against Bottoms, the Virginia Supreme Court said the child should not live with his mother because he should not have to feel the "social condemnation" that would come from living with lesbians. Bottoms's actions and abilities as a parent were not questioned by the court. Only her lesbianism was an issue.[6]

Even if relatives do not attempt to take custody of a child, lesbian and gay parents can have legal problems. The laws of many states forbid two people of the same sex from having legal custody of a child at the same time. This means that the same-sex partner of the mother or father cannot get custody even if the partner (often called a coparent) has been involved in raising the child from birth.

In most states, being in a lifelong committed relationship with a child's parent, diapering a child, rocking her when she is sick, and acting as her parent every day of her life is not enough to give a lesbian or gay parental rights. This can cause many problems for lesbian and gay families. If the biological parent dies, then the child can be taken away from the coparent—the only other caregiver the child has known. In effect, the child can lose both parents.

Battles over the family rights of lesbians and gays are continuing in the courts and legislatures. Both sides have won victories and suffered defeats. For example, the highest court in New York State has ruled that a same-sex couple can legally be defined as a family, while the Utah legislature passed a bill banning same-sex marriage.

Civil rights supporters won their greatest victory in 1993. That year, the Hawaii Supreme Court ruled that denying marriage licenses to lesbian and gay couples appeared to violate the state constitution. Although a victory, the decision did not end the argument over same-sex marriages in Hawaii. Another state court ruled that there was no compelling reason for the state to ban same-sex marriages. A statewide vote that could overturn the courts is expected in Hawaii. However, the outcome of that vote could still be challenged in court. Hawaii could still become the first state in the nation to allow lesbians and gays to legally marry. At first it even appeared that same-sex couples from other states would be able to travel to Hawaii to be married, return home and have their marriage recognized in their home states. Under the U.S. Constitution, states are supposed to recognize marriages performed in other states.

However, in 1996, civil rights opponents launched a campaign to pass laws banning same-sex marriages. Bills banning same-sex marriages were introduced in thirty-three states. Although the bills were withdrawn or defeated in seventeen states, Arkansas, Arizona, Georgia, Idaho, Kansas, Oklahoma, South Dakota, and Utah passed them. This means that even if Hawaii legalizes same-sex marriages, couples married in Hawaii will not be considered married in any of those eight states. A bill banning federal recognition of same-sex marriages passed Congress and was signed into law by President Clinton. This means that couples who are married in Hawaii will not be recognized as married by the federal government. The bill also prohibits same-sex couples from receiving any federal benefits, such as Social Security checks that surviving wives or husbands receive when their spouses die. Because they believe the proposed federal law and those already passed in many states are unconstitutional, civil rights supporters are challenging all of these laws in court.

THE EVIDENCE

Lesbian and Gay Families

Lesbian and gay families, particularly families with children, are the least visible families in the United States. Sometimes they keep themselves hidden because the parents fear losing custody of their children. Sometimes parents hide because they want to shield their children from hatred.

George B. Pyle, the editor of the *Salina Journal* newspaper in Salina, Kansas, learned about the hatred when he published a wedding announcement for two gay men in town, Steven Durant and Skip Bishop. Soon after the announcement was published and the couple were married, a rumor spread through town that the gay couple had broken up violently. The rumor claimed that one was in the hospital and the other was in jail for beating him up.

"The rumors were false," Pyle said. "Hearing them was the closest I came to feeling the hostility that Skip and Steven had to face. Many people were so offended by the idea of two men marrying each other that they actually took a morbid I-told-you-so kind of pleasure in sharing rumors of how their union ended quickly and painfully, supposedly proving that such things can't work."[7]

Civil rights opponents say that lesbians and gays do not form families like heterosexuals. According to opponents, homosexuals do not form lasting committed relationships, they do not love as heterosexuals do, and they are not loving and good parents. Because lesbian and gay families are often hidden, the truth about them and the claims of civil rights opponents can be hard to see.

Scientists in recent years, however, have uncovered new evidence about lesbian and gay families.[8] The evidence does not support any of the opponents' claims. Although it is difficult to estimate the number of committed, monogamous lesbian and gay couples, they do exist and they exist in great numbers. One study found that approximately 60 percent of lesbians and 40 percent of gay men are involved in these kinds of relationships.

Estimates on the numbers of lesbian and gay parents vary, but all studies agree that they number in the millions. One study estimated that as many as five million lesbians and three million gay men are parents. If these parents have an average of two children each, then the number of children of lesbian and gay families could be as high as fourteen million. Another study estimated that about 6 percent of the U.S. population is living in lesbian or gay families.

The quality of the relationships of lesbian and gay couples varies just like the quality of heterosexual marriages. Lesbian and gay couples can be as committed to one another and as successful in their relationship as the most loving heterosexual couples. Lesbian and gay couples can also be as unsuccessful and as unhappy as the most dysfunctional heterosexual couples.

One study used a standard test of a couple's adjustment to marriage to compare homosexual and heterosexual couples. The study could find no difference between the scores of heterosexual and homosexual couples. The same number of each group scored in the "well-adjusted" range. Another study of nearly one thousand gays and lesbians found that monogamous homosexual couples appeared happier than their heterosexual counterparts.

The evidence also suggests that the quality of parenting depends on the individual parent, not on the parent's sexual orientation. Studies suggest that lesbian mothers and gay fathers may even be more focused on their children and more sensitive to their children's needs than many heterosexual parents. Children of divorced lesbian mothers tend to have more contact with their fathers than do children of divorced heterosexual mothers. Two-mother families are especially likely to include male friends and relatives in family activities. Meanwhile, studies show that gay fathers work hard to protect their children from the hostility of others. Sometimes gay fathers send their children to schools outside of their home districts to protect them from discrimination.

There is also no evidence that lesbian and gay parents are more likely to molest their children (or their children's friends) than heterosexual parents. On the contrary, current studies show that heterosexuals are more likely to engage in the sexual abuse of children (see Chapter 4).

The Children of Lesbians and Gays

Studies have found no real difference between children raised by homosexuals and children raised by heterosexuals. Perhaps the only difference that has been noted is that the children of lesbians and gays appear to be more tolerant of differences. Children raised by lesbians and gays have been found no more likely to be homosexual than children raised by heterosexuals. The children of lesbians and gays do not have any problems that set them apart from the children of heterosexuals. Psychologist Charlotte Patterson is a leading researcher in the field.

"Although studies have assessed over 300 offspring of gay or lesbian parents in 12 different samples, no evidence has been found for significant disturbances of any kind in the development of sexual identity," Patterson said. "The same held true for moral development, intelligence, and peer relationships."[9]

Like all children, the children of lesbians and gays face problems. If their parents are divorced, then the children may blame a parent's homosexuality for the breakup of the family. Like the children of African-Americans, Native Americans, Jews, and other minorities, the children of lesbians and gays may also face prejudice. At times, they may even feel angry at their parents for being homosexual. Psychologists, however, report that this is no different than the children of heterosexuals who may feel angry about the ways in which their parents are different.

"The fact of their having some negative feelings does not mean that they are psychologically damaged by them," said psychologist April Martin. "The truth is everyone from every kind of family wishes some things were different."[10]

One teenager said, "I think growing up with lesbian parents taught me about how people can be different. And being different is just different. It isn't better or worse. I feel good about myself for understanding some things that a lot of other kids don't know. My moms have helped me a lot."[11]

Martin, a lesbian mother, says the stereotypes about lesbian and gay parents are simply not true. "People's worst fears—that our children will be harmed by teasing, shaming, or social ostracism for coming from a gay family—do not seem to be coming to pass," she said. "On the contrary, the pride we feel in our families gives our children the tools to deal with prejudice. As in any family that contains a member of an oppressed minority, our children learn to understand the problems of ignorance and bias. Depending on where they live and who they are, they make decisions about whom to tell and whom not to tell. In general, our children only rarely encounter any significant homophobic treatment. In instances when they do, they are prepared to handle it."[12]

God's Law and the Political Debate over Family

Opponents argue that God's law requires the government to deny homosexual citizens any legal acknowledgment of their families. God's law is also cited as the reason that children should be taken from their mothers and fathers.

How do you determine which version of God's law to follow? Not all religions—including all forms of Christianity—condemn marriage for lesbians and gays. (See Chapters 2 and 3 for examples of some that support same-sex marriages.) Furthermore, not all religions condemn lesbian and gay families and the efforts of homosexuals to raise their children. Which version of God's law should be followed? George Washington, Benjamin Franklin, and the other men who wrote the U.S. Constitution settled that when they declared that church and state would be separate. Under the Constitution, religion cannot be used to justify laws. (See Chapter 3 for a discussion of the separation of church and state.)

DOMESTIC PARTNERSHIPS

Under current law, a "domestic partnership" is the closest lesbian and gay Americans can come to being legally married. Domestic partnerships have been legalized in San Francisco, New York City, and about a dozen other cities.

Although the details vary from city to city, no domestic-partnership law in the country provides the same legal status to same-sex couples that marriage gives to heterosexuals. What domestic-partnership laws do is provide a public acknowledgment that a couple has pledged to live together and support each other emotionally and financially.

In most cities with domestic-partnership laws, the people who benefit the most are city employees. Under the laws, the spouse of a city employee is eligible to receive family medical insurance and any other benefits that are given to the husbands and wives of heterosexual employees. For lesbians and gays who do not work for the city, the benefits are limited. Many cities like New York offer a registry where couples can list their names after paying a fee. The laws have no impact on private businesses, taxes, rights of inheritance, or rights to visit spouses in the hospital.

Depending on the city, people qualify to be domestic partners in different ways. In San Francisco, couples qualify if they have "chosen to share one another's lives in an intimate and committed relationship of mutual care." Other ordinances require a couple to be financially responsible for one another and to have been together for a certain length of time.[13]

CHAPTER 9

BATTLEGROUND: LESBIAN AND GAY TEENS

THE ISSUES

1. Should teens be supported if they want to explore homosexuality or should they be "cured"?
2. Should progay information be available in schools?
3. Should lesbian and gay teens be allowed to socialize openly with each other in school?

THE ARGUMENTS

Teenagers must be protected from homosexuality.

1. Homosexuality is a sinful, immoral lifestyle and homosexuals lead miserable, desperate lives.
2. Teens are particularly vulnerable to "recruitment" by homosexuals and must be protected from the corrupting influence of progay materials and adult homosexuals.
3. Many homosexuals have been "cured" of the disease of homosexuality. If teenagers fall into the homosexual lifestyle, then they must be put into treatment and helped to lead healthy, moral lives.
4. If lesbian and gay teens are at high risk for suicide, it is because of the horrors of a homosexual life.

Lesbian, gay, and bisexual teens must be supported.

1. Homosexuality is not a choice. It is a difference, a normal and natural difference. It cannot nor should it be "cured."

2. Attempts to "cure" gay teens are little more than psychological and sometimes even physical torture.

3. Lesbian and gay teens must have support because they face serious problems of prejudice, discrimination, and harassment. At times, they are even rejected by their own families and forced to live on the streets.

4. The discrimination is made even worse by the fact that accurate information about adult lesbians and gays is censored. Stereotypes and lies lead teens to believe that they are doomed to lives of misery and perversion.

THE SITUATION

Although some teenagers have always identified themselves as lesbian or gay, more teens are coming out today than ever before. When the lesbian and gay civil rights movement began in the 1970s, people did not generally identify themselves as being homosexual until they were adults. On average, men came out and identified as gay when they were twenty-two, while the average age for a woman was twenty-five. Recent studies suggest, however, that the average age of coming out has fallen. In large cities, for example, the average age is now the middle to late teens. Some teenagers have reported being aware of their sexual orientation even younger.[1]

Sometimes lesbian and gay teenagers hide their orientation. Other times, they tell their family, friends, or teachers. No matter what they do, however, they are no longer invisible and alone. In the New York City public schools, for example, the Harvey Milk High School provides an education for lesbian and gay teens at high risk of dropping out. New help is also coming from groups that provide education, counseling, and support groups. Examples include Project 10 in the Los Angeles school district, the Hetrick-Martin Institute in Manhattan, Horizons Community Services in Chicago, and Passages in Kansas City. Student support groups now meet in schools in Chicago, Berkeley, Miami, Minneapolis, New York City, and many other cities. In Massachusetts alone, more than one hundred public and private schools have support groups for lesbian and gay students. Among those schools is Andover, the private school that former president George Bush attended.

In 1992, the National Education Association adopted a resolution of support for lesbian and gay students. The resolution urged schools to provide accurate information and training on gay and lesbian issues to teachers. Education officials must recognize "the right of all students to attend schools free of verbal and physical harassment, where education, not survival, is the priority."[2] In 1993, a commission appointed by Massachusetts governor William Weld, a Republican, recommended that schools protect and support lesbian and gay teenagers. Among other things, the commission recommended an end to censorship of gay and lesbian books in school libraries. Better training for teachers and school staff was also recommended.[3]

As supportive programs have grown, the opposition to them has also grown. Opponents succeeded in forcing the New York City school district to drop its plan to teach the

Rainbow Curriculum, which promoted tolerance of lesbians and gays. Soon afterwards, the New York City school superintendent was forced to resign. Groups from around the nation have succeeded in banning lesbian and gay books from school libraries. Programs such as Project 10 are constantly under attack from organizations such as the Traditional Values Coalition and the Christian Coalition. Bills have been introduced in the U.S. Congress to take away federal money from any school district that supports lesbian and gay teenagers.

THE EVIDENCE

Lesbian and Gay Teenagers

Researchers report that lesbian and gay teenagers are as normal as their heterosexual peers.[4] They mature physically in the same way. They face most of the same emotional challenges as heterosexual teenagers. Like heterosexual teens, some lesbian and gay teenagers have serious problems, while others successfully conquer the difficulties every teen faces in growing up. One study ran a series of psychological tests on two hundred lesbian and gays aged fourteen to twenty in Chicago. Researchers found that the lesbian and gay youth were normal psychologically when compared to their heterosexual peers. "These youth are neither mental patients nor runaways," the researchers wrote. "Many are in school and most of them live at home, usually with their parents."[5]

James A. Farrow, M.D., director of the Division of Adolescent Medicine at the University of Washington in Seattle, reported that most lesbian and gay youth survive adolescence without developing any problems that might bring them to the community's attention.

How Lesbian and Gay Teens Come Out

If these teenagers are no different psychologically and physically than other teenagers, then how do they know they are homosexual? Recent research has found that teenagers identify themselves as lesbian or gay because of what is inside of them—not because of something that is done to them.

Coming out as homosexual or bisexual is as natural as coming out as heterosexual, researchers report.[6] At some point in their lives, youth feel sexually attracted to certain people. For heterosexuals, the attraction is to the opposite sex. For homosexuals, the attraction is to the same sex. For bisexuals, the attraction is to both sexes. Eventually all youth explore their attraction. Sometimes the exploration is nothing more than a talk after school or a date to the movies. Sometimes it involves a kiss and sometimes—for heterosexuals, homosexuals, and bisexuals—exploration involves more, including intercourse or oral sex.

The Chicago study found that two-thirds of the two hundred youths had their first homosexual experience with peers or friends of similar ages. Their experiences were in the context of dating, childhood play, or friendship. One eighteen-year-old boy told researchers that his first homosexual experience was with a boy his own age. "It was beautiful," the boy said. "The sex wasn't planned. It was already a relationship. We'd just kissed and hugged before. I'm romantic. The relationship lasted two years. It was very romantic. I'd go to his house. We'd go out to dinner."[7]

Like heterosexual experiences, homosexual experiences vary, researchers report. Some are positive. Some are confusing or frightening. Unfortunately, some homosexual experiences, like some heterosexual experiences, occur when an adult abuses a youth. Researchers also say that homosexual youth share one other thing with heterosexual youth. Both homosexuals and heterosexuals can know their sexual orientation without ever having had a sexual experience—not even a kiss. The Chicago researchers reported that seventeen of the teenagers they studied identified themselves as lesbian or gay without ever having a sexual experience.

"These kids did not 'learn' their desires from anyone else in the simple sense," the researchers said. "They report them as being a part of their existence for as long as they can remember."[8]

The Problems of Lesbian and Gay Teenagers

Recent research suggests that lesbian and gay teenagers face a struggle that is different from that faced by heterosexual teens. For example, researchers report that lesbian and gay teens are two to three times more likely to attempt suicide than heterosexual youth.[9] One study found that the greatest danger may be in the first two years after teenagers realize that they are homosexual.

Lesbian, gay, and bisexual youths also face other problems. They are at a high risk of dropping out of school. Drinking and drug problems can occur. Young lesbians have gotten pregnant in attempts to prove that they are heterosexuals. Studies also show that teenage lesbians and gays are at greater risk than adult homosexuals and heterosexual teens for getting AIDS.

If civil rights opponents are correct, then the source of these problems is the fact that homosexuality itself is horrible. If civil rights supporters are correct, then the problems come from prejudice and lack of support. In the 1970s and even the early 1980s, few studies had been done about homosexual youth. Little evidence existed to determine whether opponents or supporters were right. However, today the situation has changed. Starting in the middle of the 1980s, a series of studies has found that the source of the problem is the rejection and hostility faced by lesbian and gay teenagers. The evidence comes from such prestigious scientific journals as *The Journal of Adolescent Health Care, Adolescent Psychiatry, Journal of Social Work and Human Sexuality, Journal of Pediatric Health Care, Journal of Consulting and Clinical Psychology*, and *The Journal of Emotional and Behavioral Problems.*[10]

Researchers have found that parents sometimes throw their lesbian and gay children out of the house. Many lesbian and gay teens report being physically attacked because of their sexual orientation. Nearly 50 percent of five hundred youths surveyed in New York City reported being attacked. More than 60 percent of those attacks occurred in their own families.

But statistics do not tell the whole story.[11] To understand what lesbian and gay youth face, think about the difference between the way people respond to them and the way they respond to heterosexual youth. When heterosexuals talk about feeling attracted to the opposite sex, adults smile and talk about how mature they are. Movies, TV shows, magazines, books, music reflect heterosexuality and endlessly discuss the joys and sorrows of heterosexual love. Church youth groups and school dances offer places for heterosexuals to meet and begin to learn how to date. Even the Homecoming Queen is expected to have a date of the opposite sex. The quarterback of the high school football team had better do the same.

When lesbian or gay youth feel attracted to the same sex, the situation is quite different. First, they may hide their feelings and sit in silence while "fag" and "dyke" jokes are told by their parents at the dinner table. News reports of the civil rights efforts by lesbians and gays may spark anger from their fathers. Mothers may mention how sorry they feel for the poor, sick homosexuals. On Sunday, teenagers may go to a church that preaches eternal damnation for homosexuals. Movies and TV seldom portray lesbians and gays positively, although portrayals of "queers" as murderers, liars, and child molesters are common.

Lesbian and gay books may not be found at the school library or, sometimes, even at the public library. One day a week may even be known as "Queer Day" at school. Anyone who wears yellow (or maybe it is green or jeans or something else) is automatically considered "queer" by students and subjected to jokes and harassment. "Fag" is the worst thing you can call someone at school. No one in the school may ever have known a lesbian or gay couple who attended a dance. But everyone may remember the poor kid who was beaten up because someone said he was gay. Teachers may know about the harassment, but seldom do anything to stop it. Sometimes the teachers are the problem.

For example, one high school gym teacher ridiculed a sixteen-year-old boy who was known to be gay. After months of harassment, the teacher made the boy attend the girls' gym class. The student complained to the principal, but no action was taken. Later the boy dropped out of school. In one school in Washington, D.C., several teachers repeatedly called an openly gay fifteen-year-old "faggot" and "fruit" at the same time that he was being harassed and beaten by students. When he complained to the principal and other teachers, they said he was the problem and recommended that he leave school.[12]

Because of all of this, lesbian and gay youth may pretend to be heterosexual. Other times, they may make their orientation known and be told that it is only a "passing phase." Other times, adults may send youth to psychologists for a cure. Parents have also been known to hold exorcisms to drive the evil of homosexuality out of their children.[13] As mentioned before, parents also throw their children out of the house. All of this damages the self-esteem of lesbian and gay youth. They can begin to believe they are the horrible monsters everyone says they are. They can be overcome with a sense of shame and hate themselves.

"Just having to listen to the ridiculing jokes or the negative stereotypes portrayed by the media takes an incredible toll on adolescent self-esteem," says James A.Farrow of the University of Washington.[14]

Shame and low self-esteem cause problems for anyone— whether heterosexual or homosexual, teenager or adult. For lesbian and gay teenagers, drugs and alcohol may seem like a way to dull the pain. Suicide may feel like a solution. Lesbian and gay youth may also become promiscuous. Sometimes they are "proving" to the world that they are the stereotype of the sex-obsessed homosexual. Sometimes they are "proving" that they are heterosexual by having intercourse with as many partners as possible.

Researchers report that one of the greatest difficulties faced by lesbian and gay teens is the fact that they are often cut off from the adult lesbian and gay communities. Lesbian and gay adults often stay away from teenagers because of fear of being accused of being child molesters and "recruiting." This leaves teens without role models or even without anyone to ask for advice. Most often, lesbian and gay teens grow up in heterosexual families, which makes the situation even more complicated.

This is a much different situation than the one faced by other minority youth. For example, an African-American teenager does not experience racism in his or her own family. A Jewish girl is not thrown out of the house because she is Jewish. Minority parents can teach their children a positive view of their own people. They can teach their children how to deal with prejudice. Too often, lesbian and gay teenagers face their problems alone.

Curing Homosexuality

As the lesbian and gay civil rights movement has grown, so have the efforts of some people to cure homosexuals. Lesbian and gay teenagers have often been the target. At times, parents have committed their children to mental institutions in an effort to change their sexual orientation. At times, teenagers themselves have asked for help.

Many people have gotten into the business of curing homosexuals. The three-hundred-member National Association for Research and Treatment of Homosexuality says that homosexuality is a treatable disorder. Other efforts to cure homosexuals are centered in the Ex-Gay Movement, which includes organizations like Exodus International. These groups are often religiously based and treat homosexuality as if it were an addiction. Through prayer and programs modeled on Alcoholics Anonymous's twelve-step program, the ex-gay groups seek either to make their participants into active heterosexuals or to make them abstain from sex.

All of these efforts have occurred despite the fact that the vast majority of American psychologists and psychiatrists do not classify homosexuality as an illness. The American Psychological Association and the American Psychiatric Association took homosexuality off the list of mental illnesses in the 1970s.

Researchers who have studied these efforts say that their ethics are questionable and the science on which they are based is "inadequate." Sometimes the therapies are abusive. Teenagers have reported being held down while hospital staff screamed at them that their homosexuality was hurting their family. Other teens report being strapped to their beds.[15]

Researchers also report that the efforts simply do not work. Bryant Welch, the American Psychological Association's executive director of professional practices, said that the therapies are "nothing more than social prejudice." A series of scientific studies has failed to provide any evidence that these methods change sexual orientation.[16]

Supporting Teens

Psychologists, psychiatrists, and social workers report that the most important thing adults can do to help lesbian and gay teens is to support them.[17] One recent study suggested that the key to lowering the suicide rate among lesbian and gay teenagers is for adults to do six things:[18]

1. Accept lesbian and gay teenagers for who they are.
2. Protect lesbian and gay teenagers from harassment and discrimination.
3. Accept lesbian and gay teenagers in their families.
4. Allow lesbian and gay teens to see positive role models of homosexual adults.
5. Give teenagers access to support groups, gaypositive therapists, lesbian and gay teen dances, and other supportive services.
6. See lesbian and gay teenagers as whole people who have both strengths and weaknesses.

CHAPTER 10
THE FUTURE

THE LEGACY OF THE PAST

In the midst of the current battle over civil rights, it is easy to forget that the public debate is only a few decades old. But even in that brief period, the lives of millions of American citizens have changed enormously.

Before the debate began in the late 1960s, police routinely raided gay bars, the only places where gays would dare to meet in public. In these raids, police would arrest anyone they could catch regardless of what the bar patrons were doing. Walking in the door of a gay bar just before a raid was enough to get someone arrested. Meanwhile, the federal government actively hunted lesbians and gays who worked in even non-military jobs. Every year thousands of law-abiding federal employees—from secretaries to scientific researchers—were fired for being homosexual.

Homosexuality was officially declared to be a mental illness by psychiatrists and psychologists. The only "help" lesbians and gays received from the mental health profession was a series of treatments that were supposed to "cure" them. These treatments included the use of nausea-producing drugs and electric shock and were sometimes so violent that they led to the death of the patient.

Devout lesbians and gays went to church and heard ministers condemn them as evil. No minister ever spoke in support of lesbians and gays and no one ever talked about the possibility that the Scripture might have been interpreted wrong. Lesbians and gays lived in fear of being discovered by other members of their congregations. If found out, homosexuals could be subject to condemnation, banishment, or even exorcism—no matter how they conducted their lives. No one had ever heard of a minister performing a same-sex marriage. For that matter, no open lesbians or gays served as clergy in any denomination anywhere in the country.

Sodomy laws were on the books in every state. These laws made it illegal for adult lesbians and gays to have sexual relations in the privacy of their own homes. Consenting adults and even couples who considered themselves to be married were made into criminals by these laws. If they were caught, they faced harsh fines and lengthy prison terms.

Laws protecting lesbians and gays from discrimination did not exist. They had never even been brought up for discussion in city councils, state legislatures, or the U.S. Congress. Not one public official ever spoke in favor of civil rights for lesbians and gays. Not one politician ever dared to make one positive statement about homosexual Americans. No business of any size prohibited discrimination against lesbian and gay employees or customers.

Meanwhile, few heterosexual Americans knew anything about lesbians and gays except for the prevailing stereotypes. Not one public figure was known to be lesbian or gay. No movie star or TV actor had ever come out to the public. No musician or singing star ever admitted it. Not one public official was known to be lesbian or gay. At the same time, few adult homosexuals dared to let even their closest heterosexual friends know that they were gay, few ever told their parents, and none came out on the job. Even lesbian and gay political organizations dared not include the words *lesbian* or *gay* in their names.

No open lesbians and gays served in the military. In fact, lesbians and gays in the military worked hard to hide their sexual orientation at the same time that the Pentagon spent hundreds of millions of dollars to find homosexuals. In the process, military police and intelligence agents hounded and harassed homosexuals and heterosexuals who were mistakenly taken to be gay. Thousands of people were given less than honorable discharges, making it harder for them to find good jobs in civilian life. Thousands of military careers were destroyed and some people were even driven to suicide. Heterosexual soldiers were demoted or harassed if they defended their gay colleagues. Lesbians and gays were sent to prison for doing nothing more than having intimate sexual relations with another adult in private.

In civilian life, lesbian and gay parents hid their sexual orientation for fear of losing custody of their children. Meanwhile, heterosexuals who were thought to be gay lost the chance to foster or adopt children because of antigay regulations.

Although many teenagers were taunted by being called "queers" and "sissies," none ever came out in school. Even if they had, lesbian and gay teens probably would not have had the support of their parents and their parents would not have had the support of groups like P-FLAG (Parents, Families, and Friends of Lesbians and Gays). Teens would have found no supportive clubs, no teacher to help, and no counselor who would have listened. No social service agencies existed outside of school to help lesbian and gay teens. If they had asked for help, they most likely would have been sent to a psychiatrist to be "cured."

Although homosexual Americans do not have equal rights with heterosexuals, they face a far different situation today than their brothers and sisters did even ten years ago. One of the most startling differences is the fact that the civil rights of lesbians and gays is being debated. Once ignored or turned into a joke, the issue of civil rights now monopolizes newspaper headlines. Millions of Americans are involved in the debate. On election day, millions base their votes on their attitudes about the issue. Millions donate money to organizations or give their time to stuff envelopes or even march in the streets to protest one action or another in the ongoing battle.

But the debate has done more than mobilize citizens to take action. It has changed laws. For example, lesbians and gays can now gather in public without the fear of arrest. Not only have police stopped raiding gay bars, but lesbians and gays have finally felt free to establish their own public institutions. For example, community centers exist in many cities. These centers host potlucks and political meetings and provide space for a variety of lesbian and gay community organizations, ranging from square dance clubs to business organizations and support groups for people who are just coming out.

Meanwhile, workers in most nonmilitary federal jobs no longer have to fear that they will be fired for being homosexual. Heterosexuals most often need not fear being mistaken for being gay. Most federal jobs are now protected by regulations that prohibit discrimination based on sexual orientation. Even though lesbians and gays are still hounded out of the military, they no longer fight alone in their battles to serve their country. New allies like the American Civil Liberties Union and other organizations now help lesbian and gay soldiers and sailors fight their dismissals. By fighting back in court, some lesbians and gays have been able to serve openly for many years.

Homosexuality is no longer considered an illness. Research led to its removal from the official diagnostic manual of the mental health profession. Meanwhile, lesbians and gays are finding support in some churches and some congregations. Several denominations, like the United Church of Christ and the Unitarian Universalists, now ordain openly lesbian and gay clergy and perform same-sex marriages. Such new denominations as the nearly all-gay Metropolitan Community Church and such organizations as the all-gay Dignity for Catholics now exist to provide a spiritual home for lesbians and gays. At the same time, even denominations that condemn homosexuality include congregations and individual clergy that support lesbians and gays. Even the fervently anti-gay Baptists include ministers who have performed same-sex marriages.

More than half of the states have repealed their sodomy laws. Laws protecting lesbians and gays from discrimination are now on the books in nine states and more than one hundred cities, towns, and counties. Although a federal antidiscrimination law has not passed, a bill to ban discrimination against homosexuals has been routinely introduced into the U.S. Congress. In 1995, President Bill Clinton became the first U.S. president to endorse one of the antidiscrimination measures when he endorsed a bill banning discrimination in employment.

More lesbian and gay parents now feel comfortable being open about their sexual orientation at the same time that more heterosexual parents are offering support to their lesbian and gay children. Although lesbian and gay teens still face many difficult problems, for the first time in history, some teens in some cities can find help. New school clubs, support groups, and social service agencies exist to help lesbian and gay teenagers accept themselves and live full and responsible lives.

The most important change for lesbian and gay Americans, however, has nothing to do with laws or legislatures. The most important change involves how lesbians and gays see themselves. Today, more and more lesbian and gay Americans have been able to shed their feelings of shame. Living openly, they nurture their families, do their jobs, go to school, and act as full partners with heterosexuals in their neighborhoods and towns. In the end, simply living unashamed and in the open may be the most revolutionary change of all for lesbian and gay Americans.

NEW ATTITUDES AND ALLIES

At the same time that lesbians and gays have changed their attitudes about themselves, an equally momentous change has occurred in the attitudes of many heterosexuals. Today an increasing number of heterosexual Americans believe they have a personal stake in the fight for civil rights for lesbians and gays. Why? The reasons vary.

An increasing number of heterosexuals believe that anti-gay laws and beliefs threaten their own families. The reason for this is simple. The vast majority of lesbians and gays are born and raised by heterosexual parents. Therefore, any legal attack on lesbians and gays hurts the children of heterosexuals. But heterosexual parents of lesbians and gays also face other problems. Discrimination and prejudice can keep their gay children from getting good jobs and confront them with violence.

Antigay discrimination and prejudice can also lead the lesbian and gay children of heterosexuals to believe that they would not be accepted if they came out to their parents. At the very least, this can lead lesbian and gay teenagers to become distant from their parents and to hide important parts of their lives. The barrier of fear and prejudice can cut teenagers off from their parents at the time when they most need their parents' guidance. At worst, the fear of rejection can drive a child to alcohol, drugs, or even suicide. Mary Griffith of Walnut Creek, California, lost her twenty-year-old son, Bobby, to suicide in 1983 after he had struggled for years with his sexual orientation. A staunch fundamentalist Christian, Mary believed that the Bible had said that homosexuality is a mortal sin and that gay people were doomed to hell.

"We were thoroughly indoctrinated to believe that as a homosexual person your way of life would be corrupt and sinful," Mary wrote in an open letter to her son published in the *San Jose Mercury News* on July 4, 1995. "As a result of these beliefs, a terrible injustice was done to you. . . . I went along in blind allegiance, unwittingly persecuting, oppressing gay and lesbian people—my own son."

Believing that her religion led her to turn away from her son when he needed her most, Mary left her church. Today, she campaigns for civil rights laws and works with parents of lesbians and gays.

An increasing number of heterosexuals believe that lesbians and gays have been used as scapegoats. The scapegoating has meant that the real causes of problems remain hidden and the solutions to the problems remain undiscovered. Labeling AIDS as a "gay disease" led authorities to ignore the growing epidemic in the 1980s. If the federal government had taken action sooner, many lives—including many heterosexual lives—might have been saved. Scapegoating lesbians and gays also leads to other problems. A gay scapegoat for the tragic accident on the battleship USS *Iowa* allowed the U.S. Navy to ignore the safety problems of the aging battleship fleet. This put thousands of heterosexual sailors in danger of being injured or killed by another accident. Scapegoating homosexuals as child molesters can lead parents to ignore the heterosexuals who are the more likely molesters. Blaming lesbians for the problem in a military unit can be a cover-up for sexual harassment. Harassing an African-American worker for being a homosexual can be a way to cover up racism in the workplace.

Many heterosexuals today believe that antigay discrimination and prejudice can lead people to act recklessly. Teenagers, for example, are at the greatest risk for self-destructive behavior. Heterosexual as well as lesbian and gay teens can feel so pressured to prove that they are "normal" that they engage in sexual intercourse before they are ready.

"The pressure to prove one's heterosexuality places young people at risk for pregnancy and sexually transmitted diseases," wrote Diane Elze, a cofounder of a Portland, Maine, support group for lesbian, gay, and bisexual youth. "In addition, AIDS-phobia has fueled homophobia and homophobia allows teens to ignore their own risk for HIV infection. A common misconception among heterosexual teens is that AIDS affects only people who are gay and IV drug users, a belief that places heterosexual teens at risk."[1]

Many heterosexuals today also believe that they, too, could easily become the target of antigay prejudice, violence, and discrimination. Writer and avowed heterosexual Cooper Thompson talked about how he felt when a gay man was murdered in the same Maine town where he lived.

"As I walked through the town, I sensed that every man in Bangor must adjust his behavior; any man was vulnerable to attack if the attackers thought he were gay," Thompson said. "About a year later, I was walking in Harvard Square in Cambridge [a place with a reputation for personal freedom] and was verbally assaulted for having my arm around another man (I was helping him through a difficult period in his life)."[2]

Heterosexuals also argue that the attacks on lesbians and gays undermine democracy and put all minorities at risk. If lesbians and gays can be excluded for being different, other minorities can also be excluded. Many of the laws and legal principles being used to attack lesbians and gays can also be used to limit the rights of other minorities.

Finally, some heterosexuals argue that the opposition to civil rights is actually only the opening shot of a much larger campaign—a campaign to limit democracy in the United States and turn it into a country where only one narrow set of beliefs and values is tolerated. Pushed by such organizations as the Christian Coalition on the religious right, this new kind of America would allegedly be based on Christian values, but the values are so narrowly defined that only Christian fundamentalists would perhaps be full citizens in this new society. All others—including many other Christians—would be excluded and perhaps even punished for their beliefs. Many (largely heterosexual) political organizations such as People for the American Way believe this larger campaign threatens to limit the freedom of all Americans. For example, when the Kansas House of Representatives passed a bill banning same-sex marriages, the small-town *Hutchinson News* said all Kansans were threatened.

"The Kansas House perhaps did not realize the gravity of what it just did," according to the newspaper's editorial. "By finagling a way to ban same-sex unions, it officially declared that people who are different, people who don't think or act like the majority, are not allowed the same rights, freedoms and privileges as the rest of Kansas citizens. Gay couples got it first. Who will be next?"[3]

Cooper Thompson is among the increasing number of heterosexuals who argue that all heterosexuals are "profoundly hurt" by prejudice (homophobia) and antigay discrimination. "The fear of being thought homosexual keeps us from being intimate with same-sex friends; the same fear can lock us into rigid definitions of masculinity and femininity," Thompson says. "Homophobia can destroy our families when we discover, and cannot accept, a family member who is lesbian, gay or bisexual. In a society where the achievements of lesbian, gay and bisexual people are hidden, we get a distorted view of reality, we learn only about the lives of other heterosexuals. The denial of equal civil rights to sexual minorities inevitably leads to limitations on the rights of all: if one group can be targeted for discrimination, any group can be targeted. In the end, homophobia prevents us from being fully ourselves."[4]

The Challenge of the Future

The final chapter in the debate over civil rights for lesbians and gays has not been written yet and will not be written for many years to come. In a very real sense, that final chapter may be written by you or by your children or by your children's children. Even if you don't want to be involved in the debate, you may not be able to avoid it. Today, everyone—from presidents to teenagers—is involved. For example, high school students in Salt Lake City found themselves in the center of the fight in 1996. That year, the Salt Lake City school board banned all after-school clubs in an effort to stop the creation of a club for lesbian and gay students. Some students took the side of the gay teens and other students opposed them. Many students walked out of school to protest the school board's action.

In the midst of all these controversies, all Americans face a challenge. Today the forces on both sides of the debate are growing in size and strength. Every victory by the supporters of civil rights prompts more people to get involved with the opponents. Every victory by opponents prompts more people to work with supporters. Neither side shows any sign of shrinking and neither shows any sign of giving up the fight or slowing down. Meanwhile, people on both sides believe they are engaged in a life and death struggle. On the surface, this would appear to be a prescription for disaster. At the very least, it could lead to the kind of violence that has already resulted in the deaths of lesbians and gays in hate crimes. At the worst, it could lead to a new civil war. What can you do?

The first step is to educate yourself. Reading this book is a good start, but you may want to learn more. It is particularly important to look for the reality underneath stereotypes. Read all sides. Weigh the evidence. Look at how the evidence was gathered and decide for yourself whether it came from a source that is likely to be accurate or a source that is likely to lie. For example, does the person providing the information have any expertise in the subject? Do these so-called experts have training that would qualify them to know what they are talking about? Do they have personal experience with what they are talking about? If these experts are scientists, do other scientists accept their work as accurate? Do other scientists criticize their methods and conclusions? If you want to know what lesbians and gays are really like, read what they say about themselves—not what somebody else says. Read more than one book or article or one source on the Internet. Remember a particular book publisher, web site, or magazine may produce materials with only one point of view.

Make up your own mind. Trust your own experience. Be open to changing your mind when you get new information and have new experiences.

Finally, treat the opposition with respect—no matter what they say about you. Whether you choose one side of the debate or the other, remember that your opponents are not demons. Treat them with the dignity that all human beings deserve. Portraying them as evil can lead to violence and make it harder to resolve the conflict. Ultimately, demonizing the opposition can only hurt democracy and lead to more conflict. Lasting solutions will come only from education and debate.

GROUPS SUPPORTING CIVIL RIGHTS

American Civil Liberties Union
132 West 43rd Street
New York, NY 10036
212/944-9800

Gay and Lesbian Alliance Against Defamation
(GLAAD)

New York: 80 Varick Street, #3E
               New York, NY 10013

San Francisco: 514 Castro Street, #B
               San Francisco, CA 94114
               415/861-4588

Gay and Lesbian Youth National Hotline
800/347-TEEN

Human Rights Campaign
1012 Fourteenth Street, N.W., #607
Washington, DC 20005
202/628-4160

Lambda Legal Defense and Education Fund
New York Office
666 Broadway
New York, NY 10012-2317
212/995-8585

National Center for Lesbian Rights
1663 Mission Street, 5th Floor
San Francisco, CA 94102
415/621-0674

National Gay and Lesbian Task Force
1734 Fourteenth Street, N.W.
Washington, DC 20009-4309
202/332-6483

P-FLAG (Parents, Families, and Friends of Lesbians
    and Gays)
1101 Fourteenth Street, N.W.
Washington, DC 20005
202/638-4200

GROUPS OPPOSING CIVIL RIGHTS

American Family Association
P.O. Box 2440
Tupelo, MS 38803
601/844-5036

The Christian Coalition
P.O. Box 1990
Cheasapeake, VA 23320
804/424-2630

Citizens for Excellence in Education
P.O. Box 3200
Costa Mesa, CA 92628
714/546-5931

Concerned Women for America
370 L'Enfant Promenade, S.W., #800
Washington, DC 20024
202/488-7000

Eagle Forum
P.O. Box 618
Alton, IL 62002
618/462-5414

Family Research Council
700 Thirteenth Street, N.W., Suite 500
Washington, DC 20005
202/393-2100

Focus on the Family
P.O. Box 35500
Colorado Springs, CO 80935
719/531-3400

Free Congress Foundation/Heritage Foundation
717 Second Street, N.E.
Washington, DC 20002
202/546-3000

Traditional Values Coalition
100 South Anaheim Boulevard, Suite 320
Anaheim, CA 92805
714/520-0300

SOURCE NOTES

INTRODUCTION: THE NEW CIVIL WAR

1. The most well-known book on the subject is James Davison Hunter's *Culture Wars: The Struggle to Define America* (Basic Books, 1991). The "holy war" comment was part of a speech Pat Buchanan made at the Republican National Convention in 1992.

2. I am indebted to Jill Pollack for providing these definitions in *Lesbian and Gay Families: Redefining Parenting in America*. (New York: Franklin Watts, 1995).

3. Family Research Institute brochure "Medical Consequences of What Homosexuals Do."

4. *The Jerusalem Post*, International Edition, May 1, 1993.

5. "Hate for the Love of God," *Topeka Capital-Journal*, July 15, 1994.

6. Richard Bernstein, "When One Person's Civil Rights Are Another's Moral Outrage," *New York Times*, October 16, 1994, p. 6.

7. Timothy Egan, "Oregon Measure Asks State to Repress Homosexuality," *New York Times*, August 16, 1992, p. 1.

8. Quote is from a 1981 fund-raising letter mailed by Falwell's "Old-Time Gospel Hour" television program, as reprinted in David E. Newton, *Gay and Lesbian Rights: A Reference Handbook* (Santa Barbara, Calif.: ABC-CLIO, 1994).

9. *Lesbian and Gay News-Telegraph* (St. Louis), February 24–March 9, 1995, p. 11.
10. Mark Thompson, *Long Road to Freedom: The Advocate History of the Gay and Lesbian Movement* (New York: St. Martin's Press, 1994), p. 228.
11. Craig Wilson, "Right Wing and Recently out of the Closet," *USA Today*, September 14, 1992, p. 4D.
12. *USA Today*, June 2, 1992, p. 10A.
13. *Kansas City Star*, September 17, 1992.

CHAPTER 1: THE STRUGGLE OVER CIVIL RIGHTS IN THE UNITED STATES

1. Among the very few exceptions were some Native American nations.
2. One of the best accounts of civil rights in the Constitution is in Ira Glasser, *Visions of Liberty: The Bill of Rights for All Americans* (New York: Arcade Publishing, 1991).
3. "Cherokee," *New Grolier Multimedia Encyclopedia,* release 6, compact disc.
4. One of the best accounts of the struggle of African-Americans is in John Hope Franklin and Alfred A. Moss, Jr., *From Slavery to Freedom: A History of Negro Americans* (New York: McGraw-Hill, 1988).
5. Historical accounts of these periods are found in John Boswell, *Same-Sex Unions in Premodern Europe* (New York: Villard Books, 1994), and Warren J. Blumenfeld and Diane Raymond, *Looking at Gay and Lesbian Life* (Boston: Beacon Press, 1993).
6. Thompson, p. 359.
7. Blumenfeld and Raymond, pp. 280–281; Martin B. Duberman, Martha Vicinus, and George Chauncey, Jr., editors, *Hidden from History: Reclaiming the Gay and*

Lesbian Past (New York: NAL Books, 1989); and Richard Plant, *The Pink Triangle: The Nazi War Against Homosexuals* (New York: Henry Holt, 1986).

8. Blumenfeld and Raymond, p. 281.

9. European Jews were the major victims of the concentration camps. An estimated six million Jews died in the Nazis' efforts to reach the "Final Solution"— a plan to destroy all of the Jewish people.

10. Blumenfeld and Raymond, p. 283; Duberman et al., p. 4; and numerous other sources.

11. Lillian Faderman, *Odd Girls and Twilight Lovers: A History of Lesbian Life in Twentieth-Century America* (New York: Penguin Books, 1991), p. 145.

12. Blumenfeld and Raymond, pp. 278, 293–295, 303–305; Jonathan Katz, *Gay American History: Lesbians and Gay Men in the USA* (New York: Avon Books, 1976), pp. 385 and 406; and Toby Marotta, *The Politics of Homosexuality* (Boston: Houghton Mifflin, 1981), p. 32.

13. Material in this section is from Gordon Allport, *The Nature of Prejudice* (Reading, Mass.: Addison-Wesley Publishing, 1954), and Blumenfeld and Raymond, pp. 214–266.

CHAPTER 2: INSIDE LESBIAN AND GAY AMERICA

1. *Topeka Capital-Journal*, October 11, 1994, p. 3A.

2. Randy Shilts, *Conduct Unbecoming: Gays and Lesbians in the U.S. Military* (New York: St. Martin's Press, 1993), p. 3.

3. Alternative (or artificial) insemination is a medical procedure that injects semen into a woman's uterus for the purpose of making her pregnant.

4. Eric Marcus, "Straight Answers," *10 Percent* magazine, Summer 1993, excerpted from *Is It a Choice? Answers to 300 of the Most Frequently Asked Questions About Gays and Lesbians* (San Francisco: Harper San Francisco, 1993), pp. 62–63.
5. Margaret L. Usdansky, "Study Fuels Homosexuality Debate," *USA Today*, August 17, 1994, p. 8A.
6. Kim Painter, "More Figures on Homosexuality," *USA Today*, October 7, 1994, p. 4D.
7. Simon LeVay and Dean H. Hamer, "Evidence for a Biological Influence in Male Homosexuality," *Scientific American*, vol. 270, no. 5 (May 1994), pp. 44–49, and Dean Hamer and Peter Copeland, *The Science of Desire: The Search for the Gay Gene and the Biology of Behavior* (New York: Simon and Schuster, 1994).
8. Associated Press, "Brain Study Finds Differences in Gays and Heterosexuals," as reported in *Lawrence* (Kansas) *Journal-World*, November 18, 1994, p. 5A; and LeVay and Hamer.
9. Blumenfeld and Raymond, pp. 85–91.
10. Gay and Lesbian Alliance Against Defamation (GLAAD), "Homophobia: Discrimination Based on Sexual Orientation," Homophobia and Violence Lesson, GLAAD/Los Angeles, 1989, curriculum material.
11. GLAAD/Los Angeles curriculum material.
12. "Klanwatch Warns of Aryan Activity," *USA Today*, March 31, 1995, p. 3A.
13. David W. Dunlap, "Survey on Slayings of Homosexuals Finds High Violence and Low Arrest Rate," *New York Times*, December 21, 1994, p. A10.
14. "Hate Crimes Get More Violent," *The* (Stamford) *Advocate*, April 18, 1995, pp. 9–10.

15. Garry Boulard, "If Words Could Kill," *The* (Stamford) *Advocate*, November 1, 1994, pp. 40–43.

16. This material was collected in private interviews with the author on October 6 and 7, 1995. To allow the people interviewed to be as open as possible, only first names are used. Although several lesbians and gays were willing to use their full names, others were not. Despite the fact that Lawrence has civil rights protection, lesbians and gays can still lose their jobs, homes, or even the custody of their children if they reveal their identities.

17. Because lesbians and gays cannot be legally married, the term *spouse* is not usually used to apply to members of a homosexual couple. Many couples today prefer the term *life partner* to show that they are committed to living together and sharing their lives.

18. Sources for this information include: Vern Bullough, *Homosexuality: A History* (New York: New American Library, 1979); Erwin Haeberle, *The Sex Atlas: A New Illustrated Guide* (New York: Continuum Publishing Co., 1982); Katz, Dolores Klaich, *Woman & Woman: Attitudes Toward Lesbianism* (New York: Simon and Schuster, 1974); David Wallechinsky, Irving Wallace, and Amy Wallace, *The People's Almanac Presents the Book of Lists* (New York: William Morrow, 1977); and Thompson.

19. American Psychological Association, "Psychology and You: Answers to Your Questions about Sexual Orientation and Homosexuality," brochure produced by APA Office of Public Affairs, 750 First Street, NE, Washington, DC 20002-4242.

CHAPTER 3: BATTLEGROUND: RELIGION

1. Advertisement placed by Coral Ridge Ministries, *USA Today*, January 18, 1995, p. 21.
2. Jeffrey H. Birnbaum, "The Gospel According to Ralph," *Time*, May 15, 1995, accessed via America Online.
3. Gustav Niebuhr, "Rev. Spong's Support of Homosexual Priests Divides Episcopalians," *Wall Street Journal*, February 20, 1991, p. 1; Peter Steinfels, "Methodist Panel Is Split on Homosexuality Issue," *New York Times*, August 28, 1991, p. A12; and David Briggs of Associated Press, "Presbyterians Vote 'No' on Sexuality Issue," reported in *Kansas City Star*, June 11, 1991, p. 1.
4. Blumenfeld and Raymond, p. 205.
5. Thompson, pp. 116, 132, and 231.
6. This is a summary of some of the points scholars make in discussing the many problems with the antigay interpretation of the story of Sodom. Blumenfeld and Raymond provided the best brief discussion of the issue. One of the most in-depth discussions of the issue is found in John McNeill, *The Church and the Homosexual*, 3rd edition (Boston: Beacon Press, 1988).
7. Bruce Hilton, *Can Homophobia Be Cured?* (Nashville: Abingdon Press, 1992), p. 69.
8. Hilton, p. 70.
9. Rev. Fred Pattison, *But Leviticus Says* (Phoenix, Ariz.: Chisto Press, 1985), as quoted in Blumenfeld and Raymond, p. 173.
10. Hilton, p. 76.
11. David Ewart, *A Scriptural View of the Moral Relations of African Slavery* (CITY: PUB, 1859) p. 12, quoted in

James O. Buswell III, *Slavery, Segregation and Scripture* (Grand Rapids, Mich.: William B. Eerdmans Publishing Co., 1964).

12. For a complete explanation of the story of Ham and related topics see Buswell's work, and Stanley Feldstein, *The Poisoned Tongue: A Documentary History of American Racism and Prejudice* (New York: William Morrow & Co., 1972).

13. Cobb, p. 3, as quoted in Buswell.

14. Arkansas Baptist resolution, quoted in E. Q. Campbell and T. F. Pettigrew, *Christians in Racial Crisis: A Study of Little Rock's Ministry* (Washington, D.C.: Public Affairs Press, 1959), p. 38.

15. Separation of church and state is discussed in what legal scholars call the "Establishment Clause" of the First Amendment. This clause declares that "Congress shall make no law respecting the establishment of religion, or prohibiting the free exercise thereof." The separation of church and state is also discussed in Article VI of the Constitution.

16. American Civil Liberties Union, "Church and State," March 22, 1995, briefing paper, accessed via America Online.

17. "Declaration of Principles," *Liberty*, November/December 1992, p. 3. It is published by the North American Division of Seventh-Day Adventists, Silver Spring, Md.

18. American Civil Liberties Union, "America's Constitutional Heritage: Religion and Our Public Schools," March 29, 1995, transcript of a video, accessed via America Online.

19. Gustav Niebuhr, "Biggest Gay Church Finds a Home in Dallas," *New York Times*, October 30, 1994, p. 10.

CHAPTER 4: BATTLEGROUND: DECRIMINALIZING HOMOSEXUALITY

1. Peter Irons, "Interview with Michael Hardwick" in William B. Rubenstein, *Lesbians, Gay Men and the Law* (New York: The New Press. 1993) pp. 125–131.

2. *Bowers v. Hardwick* case, reprinted in William B. Rubenstein, p. 143.

3. Among the many studies reporting this are: Kirkpatrick and Hitchens, "Lesbian Mothers/Gay Fathers" in P. Benedek and D. Schetky, *Emerging Issues in Child Psychiatry and The Law* (New York: Brunner/Mazel, 1985); and A. Bell and M. Weinberg, *Homosexualities: A Study of Diversity Among Men and Women* (New York: Simon and Schuster, 1978).

4. Carole Jenny, Thomas A. Roesler, and Kimberly L. Poyer, "Are Children at Risk for Sexual Abuse by Homosexuals?" *Pediatrics*, July 1994, pp. 41–44.

5. Ann Schrader, "Study: Molesters Usually Heterosexual," *Denver Post*, July 12, 1994.

6. A. Nicholas Groth, "Patterns of Sexual Assault Against Children and Adolescents" in Ann Wolbert Burgess, A. Nicholas Groth, Lynda Lytle Holmstrom, Suzanne M. Sgroi, *Sexual Assault of Children and Adolescents* (Lexington, Mass.: Lexington Books, 1978), p. 4.

7. A. Nicholas Groth and Jean Birnbaum in *Archives of Sexual Behavior*, vol. 7, no. 3, 1978.

8. "No Shield from Predators: Parent's Shouldn't Assume that Measure 9 Would Rid Schools of Potential Sexual Abusers," *The Oregonian*, September 18, 1992.

9. Keith Currey, "Divorce, Not Immorality, Biggest Threat to Families," *Christianity Today*, April 11, 1995.

10. Al Kamen, "Powell Changed Vote in Sodomy Case," *Washington Post*, July 13, 1986, p. A1.

11. Allen Ides, "*Bowers v. Hardwick*: The Enigmatic 5th Vote and the Reasonableness of Moral Certitude, *Washington and Lee Law Review*, vol. 49, no. 93 (1992), and *Washington Post*, October 26, 1990, as quoted in Rubenstein, p. 14.

12. Marshall was a key figure in the African-American civil rights movement. Among other things, he played a major role in the case of *Brown v. Board of Education*, in which the Supreme Court ruled that segregation laws are unconstitutional.

13. All of the quotes from *Bowers v. Hardwick* are from the Supreme Court opinions as reprinted in Rubenstein, pp. 132–148.

14. Among the many sources for this information are: Groth, 1978; Sandy K. Wurtele and Cindy L. Miller-Perrin, *Preventing Child Sexual Abuse* (Lincoln: University of Nebraska Press, 1992); D. J. West, *Sexual Crimes and Confrontations: A Study of Victims and Offenders* (Brookfield, Vt.: Gower Publishing Co., 1987); Jenny, 1994; and "Natural Born Predators," *U.S. News and World Report*, September 19, 1994, p. 67.

15. *U.S. News and World Report*, Sept. 19, 1994.

CHAPTER 5: BATTLEGROUND: PROTECTION FROM DISCRIMINATION

1. Linda Greenhouse, "Gay Rights Laws Can't Be Banned, High Court Rules," *New York Times*, May 21, 1996, pp. A1 and C19.

2. Greenhouse, p. C19.

3. Tony Mauro, "Supreme Court Upholds Gay Rights," *USA Today*, May 21, 1996, p. 2A.

4. Mauro, p. 2A.

5. National Gay and Lesbian Task Force Policy Institute,

"Pervasive Patterns of Discrimination Against Lesbians and Gay Men: Evidence from Surveys Across the United States," 1992.

6. Emmanuel Cleaver, mayor, "The Mayor's Commission on Lesbian and Gay Concerns, Report Summary and Overview (Kansas City, Mo.)," December 1991, pp. 6–7.

7. All examples are from a 42-page report issued by the Human Rights Campaign Fund in July 1995 and quoted by Neff, *News Telegraph*, July 14–27, 1995, pp. 3 and 13.

8. Ronald Smothers, "Company Ousts Gay Workers, Then Reconsiders," *New York Times*, February 28, 1991.

9. Neff, 13.

10. "Restaurant Bias Ban Loses," *New York Times*, November 24, 1993, p. 16.

11. Rubenstein, p. 13.

12. Neff, p. 13.

13. *National Center for Lesbian Rights* newsletter, Fall 1994, p. 9.

14. Greenhouse, p. C19.

15. *Romer v. Evans*, preliminary printing of the *United States Reports*, accessed via America Online, May 20, 1996, section II.

16. *Romer v. Evans*, section II.

17. *Romer v. Evans*, section III.

18. Jean E. Dubofsky, counsel of record, *Romer v. Evans*, Supreme Court of the United States, October Term, 1994, p. 49, brief for respondents.

19. Richard Bernstein, "When One Person's Civil Rights Are Another's Moral Outrage," *New York Times*, October 16, 1994, p. 6E.

20. Decision in *Romer v. Evans*, Supreme Court, State of Colorado, Nos. 94SA48 and 94SA128, Oct. 11, 1994, accessed via America Online.

21. Lambda Legal Defense and Education Fund, "LLDEF Background Briefing: Colorado's Anti-Gay Amendment 2, Organizations Signing on As Amicus Before U.S. Supreme Court in Opposition to Colorado's Anti-Gay Ballot Initiative," June 19, 1995.

22. J. Clay Smith Jr., counsel of record, National Bar Association, Brief for Amicus Curiae National Bar Association in Support of Respondents, June 1995, p. 9.

23. *Newsweek*, September 14, 1992, pp. 36–37.

24. Human Rights Campaign, "President Endorses Employment Non-Discrimination Act," October 20, 1995, press release.

25. Thompson, p. 344.

26. Thompson, p. 393.

27. National Gay and Lesbian Task Force, Workplace Initiative Project, updated June 1994.

28. Tom Webb, "Group Polls Congress on Hiring of Gays," *Wichita Eagle*, June 26, 1994; and Human Rights Campaign, October 20, 1995.

29. Joyce Purnick, "Gay Rights Looking Back at a Non-Crisis," *New York Times*, March 21, 1996.

30. Purnick.

CHAPTER 6: BATTLEGROUND: THE MILITARY

1. "Defense Force Management: DoD's Policy on Homosexuality," U.S. Government Accounting Office, June 1992.

2. Shilts, 1993, pp. 639–640.

3. The best accounts of the investigations are found in Shilts, 1993; and in news reports like "Conduct Unbecoming by Whom?" *Time*, November 29, 1993.

4. Shilts, 1993, p. 476.

5. Shilts, 1993, pp. 436–437, 585.
6. One of the best histories of lesbians and gays in the U.S. military is in Shilts, 1993.
7. Many books have covered the subject in detail. They include: Shilts, 1993; Allen Berube, *Coming out Under Fire: The History of Gay Men and Women in World War Two* (New York: The Free Press, 1990); J. Harry, "Homosexual Men and Women Who Served Their Country," *Journal of Homosexuality*, 1984, pp. 117–125; M. Hippler, *Matlovich: The Good Soldier* (Boston: Alyson Press, 1989); and M. A. Humphrey, *My Country, My Right to Serve: Experiences of Gay Men and Women in the Military, World War II to the Present* (New York: HarperCollins, 1990).
8. Shilts, 1993, p. 282.
9. Thompson, p. 360.
10 African-Americans fought in all-black units until 1948, when President Harry Truman issued an order integrating the armed services.
11. Patrick Pexton, "16 Homosexuals Serve Legally, Openly," *Air Force Times*, March 27, 1995.
12. The all-female branches of the U.S. military were created during World War II. They were the Women's Army Corps. (WAC), Women's Air Force (WAF), and the Women's Auxiliary Volunteer Emergency Service (WAVES). They were disbanded between 1973 and 1978.
13. Shilts, 1993, pp. 315–318, 495–496.
14. Shilts, 1993, p. 539.
15. Shilts, 1993, p. 475.
16. Nancy Gibbs, "Marching out of the Closet," *Time*, August 19, 1991; Clarence Page, "Why Does the Military Still Ban Homosexuals?" *Kansas City Star*, February 15, 1991; and Shilts, 1993, p. 726.

17. Among the best accounts of Perry Watkins's Army career are in Shilts, 1993, and Rubenstein, pp. 342–367.

18. Shilts, 1993, p. 242.

CHAPTER 7: BATTLEGROUND: AIDS AND GAY RIGHTS

1. A small minority of physicians believe that HIV is not the primary cause of AIDS. However, the majority of scientists and physicians disagree with their findings and say that all the evidence points to HIV as the cause of the disease.

2. Semen is the whitish fluid filled with sperm that is ejaculated out of a man's penis when he has an orgasm. Vaginal fluids are secreted by a woman's genitals.

3. A condom is a latex sheath that a man may wear over his penis during intercourse. A dental dam is a square of latex that can be used to protect a person's mouth while he or she is performing oral sex on his or her partner. The dental dam is put over the mouth to form a barrier between the mouth and semen or vaginal fluids. The latex squares are called dental dams because they were first used by dentists in their work.

4. Thompson, p. 245.

5. Ronald Godwin, "AIDS: A Moral and Political Time Bomb," *Moral Majority Report,* vol. 2 (July 1982).

6. Laurie Garrett provides the best explanation of the theories in *The Coming Plague: Newly Emerging Diseases in a World Out of Balance* (New York: Farrar, Straus and Giroux, 1994), pp. 281–389.

7. Garrett, p. 364.

8. The best discussions of the spread of AIDS are in Garrett

and Randy Shilts, *And the Band Played On: Politics, People and the AIDS Epidemic* (New York: St. Martin's Press, 1987).

9. The meeting took place in January 1983 and has been reported in detail in Garrett, pp. 311–315; and Shilts, 1987, pp. 220–224.

10. Garrett, p. 303.

11. Garrett, p. 301.

12. Blumenfeld and Raymond, pp. 330–331.

13. Shilts, 1987, p. 95.

14. Blumenfeld and Raymond, pp. 333–334.

15. "AIDS," *Compton's Encyclopedia*, accessed via America Online in September 1995.

16. "Big Increase in Heterosexual AIDS Cases," *Chicago Tribune*, March 11, 1994.

17. Suzy Frisch, "State Says More at AIDS Risk," *Chicago Tribune*, February 4, 1995.

18. "Africa: Education and Health," *Compton's Encyclopedia*, accessed via America Online.

19. "Dangerous Sex: New Signs of Risk Taking Prompt Rethinking About AIDS Prevention," *Scientific American*, February 1995, p. 10.

20. John Crewdson, "Measuring the AIDS Threat," *Chicago Tribune*, February 6, 1994.

21. John C. Gonsiorek and Michael Shernoff, "AIDS Prevention and Public Policy: The Experience of Gay Males," *Homosexuality: Research Implications for Public Policy* (Newbury Park, Calif.: Sage Publications, 1991).

22. Judy Plunkett Evans, "Going Public," *Chicago Tribune*, September 27, 1994.

23. *Chicago Tribune*, December 23, 1994.

24. "Milestones," *Time*, December 8, 1994.

CHAPTER 8: BATTLEGROUND: LESBIAN AND GAY FAMILIES

1. David W. Dunlap, "Some States Trying to Stop Gay Marriages Before They Start," *New York Times*, March 15, 1995, p. A10.
2. Dunlap.
3. Social Security is a federal program that provides financial help to people in certain situations. A surviving spouse in a heterosexual marriage gets a Social Security check. People also receive Social Security payments when they retire or if they suffer a disability.
4. *Newsweek*, September 14, 1992, p. 37.
5. Signed by both of them, Sharon Bottoms and April Wade's vows read: "I promise to be faithful, honest and totally yours, for as long as I shall love. . . . I ask that you take me as I will take you, to love and cherish forever in life, till death do us part." See William A. Henry III, "Gay Parents: Under Fire and on the Rise," *Time*, September 9, 1993.
6. "A Case of Justice Gone Badly Awry," *Chicago Tribune*, May 6, 1995, editorial.
7. George B. Pyle, "For Better, For Worse," *Salina Journal* November 2, 1993, p. 5.
8. The best descriptions of these studies can be found in Blumenfeld and Raymond, pp. 386–387. Other resources are Charlotte Patterson, "Children of Lesbian and Gay Parents," *Child Development*, vol. 63 (1992), pp. 1025–1042; American Bar Association study, 1988; *Introduction to Lesbian Families*, published by the Lavender Families Resource Network; and Frederick W.

Bozett, "Children of Gay Fathers," in *Gay and Lesbian Parents* (New York: Praeger, 1987), p. 45.

9. Patterson, 1992.

10. April Martin, *The Lesbian and Gay Parenting Handbook* (New York: HarperPerennial, 1993), p. 26.

11. Martin, p. 26.

12. Martin, p. 26.

13. Pollack, p. 90; Jane Gross "After a Ruling Hawaii Weighs Gay Marriages," *New York Times*, April 25, 1994, p. A1; and Jean Seligmann, "Variations on a Theme," *Newsweek*, Special Edition: The 21st Century Family, Winter/Spring 1990, p. 38.

CHAPTER 9: BATTLEGROUND: LESBIAN AND GAY TEENS

1. Gilbert Herdt and Andrew Boxer, *Children of Horizons* (Boston: Beacon Press, 1993), p. 6.

2. The National Education Association is the largest teachers' union in the country. This information is from the NEA, "Equal Access Fact Sheet on Teaching and Counseling Gay and Lesbian Students," 1992.

3. "Tune In, Come Out," *Newsweek*, November 8, 1993, pp. 70–71.

4. This material is from several studies, including Ritch Savin-Williams, "An Exploratory Study of Pubertal Maturation Timing and Self-Esteem Among Gay and Bisexual Male Youths," *Developmental Psychology*, January 1995, pp. 56–64, and James A. Farrow, "Gay and Lesbian Youth Suicide," *Focal Point*, Spring/Summer 1991.

5. Herdt and Boxer, p. xiv.

6. One of the most complete studies of the coming-out

process of teenagers is in chapters 4 and 5 of Herdt and Boxer.

7. Herdt and Boxer, p. 189.

8. Herdt and Boxer, pp. 186–187.

9. Studies outlining the problems of lesbian and gay teens include Paul Gibson, "Gay and Lesbian Youth Suicide," U.S. Department of Health and Human Services Youth Suicide Report 110, 1989; C. D. Proctor and V. K. Groze, "Risk Factors for Suicide Among Gay, Lesbian and Bisexual Youths," *Social Work*, vol. 39, no. 5 (1994), pp. 504–512; Gary Remafedi, James Farrow, and Robert Deisher, "Risk Factors for Attempted Suicide in Gay and Bisexual Youth," *Pediatrics*, June 1991, pp. 869–875; and Susan Messina, "Lesbian, Gay and Bisexual Youth: At Risk and Underserved," The Center for Population Options, Washington D.C., September 1992.

10. Among the studies are: Proctor and Groze; J. Gonsiorek, "Mental Health Issues of Gay and Lesbian Adolescents," *Journal of Adolescent Health Care*, no. 9, pp. 114–122; A. Soundheimer, "Anticipation and Experimentation: The Socialization of the Gay Adolescent," *Adolescent Psychiatry*, no. 10, pp. 52–62; T. A. DeCrescenzo, "Homophobia: A Study of Attitudes of Mental Health Professionals Toward Homosexuality," *Journal of Social Work and Human Sexuality*, no. 2, pp. 115–136; R. J. Bidwell, "The Gay and Lesbian Teen: A Case of Denied Adolescence," *Journal of Pediatric Health Care*, no. 2 (1988), pp. 3–8; Ritch Savin-Williams, "Verbal and Physical Abuse As Stressors in the Lives of Lesbian, Gay Male and Bisexual Youths," *Journal of Consulting and Clinical Psychology*, vol. 62, no. 2, April 1994, pp. 261–269; Jill Gover, "Gay Youth

in the Family," *Journal of Emotional and Behavioral Problems,* vol. 2, no. 4, Winter 1994, pp. 34–38; Joyce Hunter, "Violence Against Lesbian and Gay Male Youths," *Journal of Interpersonal Violence,* September 1990, pp. 295–300; and Ritch C. Savin-Williams, "Theoretical Perspectives Accounting for Adolescent Homosexuality," *Journal of Adolescent Health Care,* 1988, pp. 95–103.

11. One of the best explorations of the difficulties faced by lesbian and gay teens is Kurt Chandler and Rita Reed, "Growing up Gay," *Minneapolis Star Tribune,* special section, December 6, 1992.

12. Donna Dennis and Ruth Harlow, "Gay Youth and the Right to Education," *Yale Law and Policy Review,* no. 4 (1986).

13. Some people believe that an evil, supernatural spirit can possess and take over the mind and soul of a human being. An exorcism is a ritual used to drive the evil spirit out of the person.

14. Farrow, 1991.

15. Bruce Mirken, "Setting Them Straight," *10 Percent* magazine, June 1994, pp. 57–58.

16. Quoted in Douglas C. Haldeman, "Sexual Orientation Conversion Therapy for Gay Men and Lesbians: A Scientific Examination," in *Homosexuality: Research Implications for Public Policy* (Newbury Park, California: Sage Publications, 1991), pp. 149–160.

17. Among the studies showing this are Sue Kiefer Hammersmith and Martin S. Weinberg, "Homosexual Identity: Commitment, Adjustment and Significant Others," *Sociometry,* vol. 36, no. 1 (1973); Alan P. Bell and Martin S. Weinberg, *Homosexualities: A Study of Diversity*

Among Men and Women (New York: Simon and Schuster, 1978); and Ritch C. Savin-Williams, "Parental Influences on the Self-Esteem of Gay and Lesbian Youths," *Journal of Homosexuality*, vol. 17 (1989), pp. 93–100.

18. This list comes from E. E. Jacobsen, "Lesbian and Gay Adolescents: A Social Work Approach," *The Social Worker Le Travailleur*, Summer 1988, pp. 65–67.

CHAPTER 10: THE FUTURE

1. Diane Elze, "It Has Nothing to Do with Me," in Warren J. Blumenfeld, ed., *Homophobia: How We All Pay the Price* (Boston: Beacon Press, 1992, p. 99).
2. Cooper Thompson, "Heterosexual in a Homophobic World," Blumenfeld p. 241.
3. "The Easy Way Out," *Hutchinson* (Kansas) *News*, March 24, 1996, editorial.
4. Thompson, pp. 239–240.

FOR MORE INFORMATION

READING

Benkov, Laura. *Reinventing the Family: The Emerging Story of Lesbian and Gay Parents*. New York: Crown Publishers, 1994.

Brimner, Larry Dane. *Being Different: Lambda Youths Speak Out*. Danbury, Conn.: Franklin Watts, 1995.

Burke, Phyllis. *Two Moms and Their Son*. New York: Random House, 1993.

Chauncey, George. *Gay New York: Gender, Urban Culture, and the Making of the Gay Male World, 1890–1940*. New York: Basic Books, 1994.

Curry, Hayden and Denis Clifford. *A Legal Guide for Lesbian and Gay Couples*. Berkeley, Calif.: Nolo Press, 1993.

Dew, Robb Forman. *The Family Heart: A Memoir of When Our Son Came Out*. Reading, Mass.: Addison-Wesley, 1994.

Hartman, Keith. *Congregations in Conflict: The Battle Over Homosexuality*. New Brunswick, N.J.: Rutgers University Press, 1996.

Martin, April. *The Lesbian and Gay Family Handbook*. New York: HarperPerennial, 1993.

McCuen, Gary E., ed. *Homosexuality and Gay Rights.* Hudson, Wis.: G. E. McCuen Publications, 1994.

Mickens, Ed. *The 100 Best Companies for Gay Men and Lesbians.* New York: Pocket Books, 1994.

Nava, Michael. *Created Equal: Why Gay Rights Matter to America.* New York: St. Martin's Press, 1994.

Pollack, Jill S. *Lesbian and Gay Families: Redefining Parenting in America.* Danbury, Conn.: Franklin Watts, 1995.

Pollack, Rachel. *The Journey Out: A Book for and about Gay, Lesbian, and Bisexual Teens.* New York: Viking, 1995.

Signorile, Michelangelo. *Queer in America: Sex, the Media, and the Closets of Power.* New York: Anchor Books, 1994.

Slater, Suzanne. *The Lesbian Family Life Cycle.* New York: Free Press, 1995.

White, Mel. *Stranger at the Gate: To Be Gay and Christian in America.* New York: Simon and Schuster, 1994.

Swisher, Karin L., ed. *Teenage Sexuality: Opposing Viewpoints.* San Diego: Greenhaven Press, 1994.

ORGANIZATIONS

Bisexual Resource Center
P.O. Box 639
Cambridge, MA 02140
617/424-9595
E-mail: brc@norn.org

Gay and Lesbian Alliance Against Defamation (GLAAD)
8455 Beverly Boulevard, Suite 305
Los Angeles,CA 90048
213/658-6775

Gay and Lesbian Parents Coalition International
P.O. Box 50360
Washington, DC 20091

International Association of Lesbian/Gay Pride Cooordinators,
Inc.
584 Castro Street, Suite 513
San Francisco, CA 94114
E-mail: ialgpc@tde.com
Web page: http://www.tde.com/~ialgpc

Lesbian and Gay Community Services Center
208 West 13th Street
New York, NY 10011
212/620-7310

Men of All Colors Together
7985 Santa Monica Boulevard, Suite 109-136
West Hollywood, CA 90046
213/664-4716

National Center for Lesbian Rights
1663 Mission Street, Suite 550
San Francisco, CA 94103

National Latino/a Lesbian and Gay Organization
703 G Street, S.E.

Washington, DC 20003
202/544-0092

National Lesbian & Gay Health Association
1407 S Street, N.W.
Washington, DC 20009
202/939-7880

World Congress of Gay and Lesbian Jewish Organizations
P.O. Box 3345
New York, NY 10008-3345

INTERNET SITES

Gay and Lesbian Info
Hundreds of links to every imaginable gay-and-lesbian-related site
http://www.ping.be/~ping1678/gay.htm#WEB

Gay and Lesbian Resources
Links to other sites, magazines, mailing lists, news, resources
http://www.3wnet.com/reference/gnl.html

Gay/Lesbian Jewish Organizations
Connect with Jewish groups in Dallas, San Antonio, New York, Chicago, Long Beach (Calif.), Montreal, Toronto, and the Netherlands
http://members.gnn.com/EtzChaim/sister1.htm

GayNet
Free software, chat groups, and lots more
http://www.gay.net/

A Gay Place in Cyberspace
Travel, shopping, news, gossip
http://www.maui.net/~randm/gp.html

Gayweb
News, products, software, videos, etc.
http://www.gayweb.com/

International Gay and Lesbian Outdoor Organizations
Trips and sports organizations in the United States, Puerto
Rico, Canada, France, Australia, Germany, Japan, New
Zealand, Great Britian, and South Africa
http://www.chiltern.org/chiltern/igloo.html

OrgsToGo
Links to hundreds of lesbian, gay, and bisexual organizations
and centers
http://www.gaybiznet.com/otg.html

Qworld
Chat areas, message boards, magazines, contests, shopping,
and more
http://www.qworld.org/

INDEX

Abzug, Bella, 83
Acquired Immune Deficiency Syndrome (AIDS), 97, 106, 111–123, 141, 153, 154
AIDS Project/LA, 115
African-Americans, 23–26, 33–34, 51, 64–65, 82, 91, 93, 94, 105, 109, 125, 132, 145, 154
Alexander the Great, 102
Allen, Ernie, 79
Amedure, Scott, 45
Amendment 2, 47, 84–85, 87, 88–89, 92–94, 116
American Civil Liberties Union, 30, 150
American Psychiatric Association, 31, 53, 145
American Psychological Association, 52–53, 90–91, 145, 146
Americans with Disabilities Act, 116
American Theological Society's Committee on Sexuality, 59

America Online's Gay and Lesbian Community Forum, 66
Andover School, 38
Ardolino, Emile, 123
Ashman, Howard, 52
Asian-Americans, 26, 34, 93
Auden, W.H., 52

Ben-Shalom, Miriam, 99
Bernstein, Leonard, 52
Bill of Rights, 21–22, 23, 35, 36, 80
Birnbaum, Jean, 73, 74
Bishop, Skip, 129–30
Blackmun, Harry, 72, 76, 77
Bottoms, Sharon, 127
Bottoms, Tyler, 127
Bowers v. Hardwick, 32, 69, 71, 72, 75–77, 80, 81, 85, 91–92
Bray, Robert, 126
Brenner, Claudia, 46
Bridges, William A., 86
Britten, Benjamin, 52
Brown v. Board of Education, 25

Bryant, Anita, 31
Bush, George, 116, 120, 138

Cameron, Paul, 90
Cammermeyer, Margarethe, 103
Campolo, Tony, 75
Cather, Willa, 52, 83
Centers for Disease Control, 118, 119
Child molesters, 68, 72, 73–74, 78–78, 89, 90, 131–32, 144, 154
Christian Coalition, 56, 139, 155
Christianity, 26, 37, 54–67, 69, 72–74, 91, 95, 111, 115, 121, 125, 133–34, 147–48, 151, 153
Christina (queen of Sweden), 52
Civil Rights Act, 1964, 82, 88
Clift, Montgomery, 52
Clinton, Bill, 95, 98, 99, 129, 151
Cobb, Howell, 64
Coles, Matt, 88
Coming out, 38, 43–45, 140–41, 148
Constitution, U.S., 21–22, 23, 24, 65, 69, 72, 75, 76, 77, 80, 87–88, 128, 134
Copeland, Aaron, 51
Cracker Barrel Country Store and Restaurant chain, 86–87

Daughters of Bilitis, 29
Decatur, Stephen, 102
Deitrich, Marlene, 52
Dignity for Catholics, 67, 151
Diya, Angela, 122
Dressel, Jim, 103
Durant, Steven, 129–30

Edwards, Edwin, 94
Ellis, Perry, 123
Elze, Diane, 154
Etheridge, Melissa, 52
Evangelicals Concerned, 67
Ewart, David, 64
Ex-Gay Movement, 145
Exodus International, 145

Family Research Council, 126
Family Research Institute, 90
Farrow, James A., 139, 144
Feldblum, Chai, 85
Finlater, W.W., 66
Forster, E.M., 52
Frank, Barney, 38
Frederick II (king of Prussia), 102

Gay Games, 47
Gay Men's Health Crisis, 115, 121
Gays and lesbians
    discrimination and prejudice against, 33–34, 36, 43, 45–47, 68–77, 80–97, 101, 106–

7, 119–20, 133, 141–
42, 144, 145, 146,
147, 151, 152, 154,
156, 157
families, 37, 39, 49, 92–
93, 124–35, 149
in history, 26–29, 51–
52, 102–3
and the military, 38, 97–
110, 147, 149, 150,
154
and religion, 26, 37,
54–67, 68, 69, 72–
74, 91, 92, 95, 111,
115, 122, 125, 133–
34, 147–48, 151, 153
teenagers, 136–46, 149
Glaser, Ariel, 122
Glaser, Elizabeth, 122
Glaser, Jake, 122
Glaser, Paul Michael, 122
Goldberg, Suzanne, 92
Greenhouse, Linda, 84, 85
Griffith, Bobby, 153
Griffith, Mary, 153
Groth, A. Nicholas, 73, 74
Gunderson, Steve, 38

Hall, Brian, 122
Hardwick, Michael, 71
Harvey Milk High School,
138
Hay, Henry, 29
Hetrick-Martin Institute, 96,
138
Hilton, Bruce, 61
Hispanic Americans, 26, 93

Horizons Community Ser-
vices, 138
Howard, Charles, 46
Howard, John, 86
Hudson, Rock, 52, 115
Human Immunodeficiency
Virus (HIV), 113, 114,
115, 116, 117, 118, 121,
154

Is it a Choice? (Marcus), 40
Islam, 58–59

Jantz, Vernon, 86, 87–88
Jenny, Carole, 73
Jews, 26, 28, 34, 41, 54, 58,
63, 132, 145
John, Elton, 52
Johnson, Earvin "Magic,"
113
Johnson, Owen, 110

Kennedy, Anthony M., 84,
88–89
King, Martin Luther, Jr., 51
Kinsey Alfred, 40–41
Klanwatch, 46
Koop, C. Everett, 120
Kritsick, Stephen M., 123
Kuehl, Sheila James, 38–39
Kunreuther, Frances, 96

Lambda Legal Defense and
Education Fund, 92
Leadership Conference on
Civil Rights, 95
Lee, Wayne, 45–46

Leonardo da Vinci, 52
Lesbian and Gay Rights Project of the American Civil Liberties Union, 88
Lesbians. *See* Gays and lesbians
Liberty, 66
Lippert, Patrick, 123
Louganis, Greg, 113
Lyon, Phyllis, 29

Martin, April, 133
Martin, Del, 29
Matlovich, Leonard, 99, 103
Mattachine Society, 29
Mauro, Tony, 85
Mercury, Freddie, 123
Michelangelo, 52
Moral Majority, 116
Moss, Andrew, 119–20

National AIDS Commission, 120
National Association for Research and Treatment of Homosexuality, 145
National Association for the Advancement of Colored People Legal Defense and Education Fund, 93
National Center for Missing and Exploited Children, 79
National Coming Out Day, 38
National Gay and Lesbian Task Force, 85–86, 95, 126

Native Americans, 22–23, 26, 132
Nazi Germany, 27–29, 34, 51
Newak, Joann, 101
Nickerson, Eugene H., 101

O'Donovan, Jerome, 96
Osburn, C. Dixon, 105

Palomo, Juan R., 47
Parental rights, 92–
Passages, 138
Patterson, Charlotte, 132
Pattison, Fred, 63
People for the American Way, 155
Perciballi, Joyce, 86
Peters, Michael, 123
Pfeegeer, David, 67
P-FLAG (Parents, Families and Friends of Lesbians and Gays), 149
Phelps, Fred, 57
Plessy v. Ferguson, 25
Powell, Lewis F., 75–76
Priest, Josiah, 64
Project,10, 138, 139
Pruitt, Dusty, 108
Purnick, Joyce, 95
Pyle, George B., 129–30

Rainbow Curriculum, 139
Reagan, Ronald, 84, 119, 120
Richard the Lion-Hearted (king of England), 52, 102
Romer v. Evans, 84–85, 88

Rosanbalm, Jerry, 102–3
Rustin, Bayard, 51

Salk Institute for Biological Studies, 42
Same-sex marriages, 32, 35, 36, 54, 55, 59, 70, 124, 125, 126, 128–29, 133, 148, 151, 155–56
Scientific Humanitarian Committee, 29
Segregation, 24–25, 34, 64, 65, 69, 105
Servicemembers Legal Defense Network, 105
Shanti Project, 115, 121
Shilts, Randy, 38, 103, 120
Sipple, Oliver "Bill," 51
Slavery, 20, 23, 24, 64–65, 69, 75
Smith, Bessie, 52
Society for Human Rights, 29
Socrates, 52
Sodomy laws, 32, 60, 68–77, 85, 91–92, 148, 151
Somers, Richard, 102
Spong, John Shelby, 56
Star, Paul, 101
Stein, Gertrude, 52
Stevens, John P., 76, 77, 84
Stonewall Rebellion, 30–31, 47
Suicide, 136, 141, 144, 146, 153
Summerville, Cheryl, 87

Supreme Court, U.S., 25, 32, 45, 72, 75–77, 80, 82, 84–85, 87–89, 91, 93, 99, 110

Tchaikovsky, Peter Ilyich, 52
Thomas, Clarence, 84
Thompson, Cooper, 154–55, 156
Traditional Values Coalition, 56, 139
Turing, Alan, 51

Universal Fellowship of Metropolitan Community Churches, 37, 67, 151

von Steuben, Frederich, 102

Wade, April, 127
Washington, George, 21, 102, 134
Watkins, Perry, 109–10
Welch, Bryant, 146
West, Nicholus, 47
White, Patrick, 52
Whitman, Walt, 52
Wight, Rebecca, 46
Williams, Tennessee, 52
Winn, Don, 103
Women's rights, 20, 22, 82, 93
Woolf, Virginia, 52

Zamora, Pedro, 123